2023

MW01273434

You Only Die Once

How Riding a Bicycle Across
America taught me to live.
Right. Now.

To Karen from Renee

Jillyn Hawkley Peterson

DRABATIC PRESS, LLC

YOU ONLY DIE ONCE

ISBN: 978-0-9852102-9-8 (Paperback)

Library of Congress Control Number: 00000000000

This is a write-up of events as they happened to the best of my memory or as they have been retold to me. Some names and events have been omitted to facilitate the story and some have been adapted to avoid confusion. Photographs were taken by Randy Peterson.

Front cover image design by Jill Peterson and Hector Epaminondas.

Book design by Drabatic Press.

Printed by Drabatic Press, Inc., in the United States of America.

First printing edition 2019.

www.JypsyJillRides.com

www.DrabaticPress.com

INTENTIONAL READER GUIDE:

Note: this is, as far as we at Drabatic Press know, the first reader guide of its kind. We are indebted to the video filtering company VidAngel (vidangel.com) for the idea. We believe the industry standard categories of MG/YA/Adult to be totally inadequate as a means of determining whether a book is suited to the reader. Readers young and not-as-young need to know more precisely what kinds of content they are about to consume.

Accordingly, at the front of each of our books, readers will find a reader guide, outlining in detail the sort of material that can be found in the work. We hope this will be helpful, even if there are necessarily some minor spoilers involved.

~Drabatic Press

POTENTIALLY OBJECTIONABLE CONTENT:

Swearing: I do say "hell" twice, and "damn" once, neither gratuitously.

Mature Activities: Chapter Eight discusses the impact on the friends and family of James McFee, who died by suicide.

Intimate Contact: None

Violence: I did have a potentially harmful situation on the road, but it shouldn't scare anyone very badly other than my mother.

Intensity: Occasional discussion of intense moments for *me*, but mostly they won't make *your* heart beat any faster. Again, unless you're my mom. Don't forget, mom. I'm still alive.

General Age Range: 8 years and up—although we believe that none of the material in this book would be inappropriate for a reader of any age.

You Only Die Once

Being aware of the present moment simply means you never believe the illusion that the future is going to be better than what is going on right now.

Plan, dream, and organize all you want; just don't start believing that what you have planned for the future is going to be any better than your current moment. You are going to be in the present moment your entire life. If you are focusing on how good the future (that really doesn't exist) is going to be, you are just running the hamster wheel hoping to get somewhere.

Life is right now, in this glorious moment right in front of you. I believe that if you are not allowing yourself to be happy right NOW, nothing external in the future is going to change that permanently."

-Mateo Tamatabai, *The Mind-Made Prison: Radical Self-help and Personal Transformation*

Please note: The chapters in this book count down instead of up, as did the miles between Westport and Key West to Mile Marker 0.

Epilogue, Dedication, and Acknowledgments

With every broken bone, I swear, I lived.

- One Republic, "I Lived"

The two most common questions when I told people I was riding a bicycle from coast to coast were, "WHY?" and, "Doesn't your butt hurt?"

The answer to the latter is—of course. At some point I realized/remembered that pain is not the enemy. Every time I get on the bike, for the first mile or so before I'm fully "warm," all my muscles are firing at 100%. I'm excited and happy to be on the bike. Typically, right around the end of the first mile, there is a tendon in my thigh that starts to get tight—and has a dull ache. If I go into my second mile without that particular tendon starting to ache, I will start trying to figure out what is wrong. I get *uncomfortable* with how comfortable it is. Uncomfortable has truly become my comfort zone.

The answer to the first is a little more complicated; being that it started for one reason and developed additional reasons along the way. Perhaps the best explanation would be that you hold the reasons in your hand.

In Chapter Two I mention Aaron Batteen and his wife, Lindsey and their three children. Aaron passed away tragically on November 15, 2019, just seven months after they co-hosted a surprise birthday party for me while I was on the ride, and four months after Lindsey gave birth to their fourth child. Aaron was one of the most genuinely kind people I've ever known, and one of the people who lived his life enjoying the ride. He loved his wife and his children with everything he had, and everything he was. Even after a severe injury and emergency surgery, he loved God and loved his life despite sub-optimal circumstances. The day before he passed he conveyed a level of gratitude for this life and joy that is an exemplary reminder to me every day since. Aaron was dearly, dearly loved and will be missed deeply.

And you, dear reader, are as well. I am dedicating this book to you—whoever and wherever you are in your particular journey. Thank you for joining a piece of mine. Hopefully the stories will bring you a smile or two, a little insight into the mind of an endurance athlete, and the inspiration to know that you can—and *do*—do hard things every day, and that you can also enjoy the ride.

Unending gratitude to the following—my dearest husband, Randy, who has shown me the world and continues to fund and prompt my dreams; Rachel and d'Artagnan, the most amazing kids; James McFee, even though he's a punk, but had the foresight before leaving this life to introduce me to Pam Bradley and Brooke McMillion, as well as his mother, Linda, all of whom deserve the best that life has to offer; my dear friends Chris and Jeanette Jones and their family, for giving me a safe space to harbor a pretty wicked storm; Dawn Ralston and Charmaine Fletcher, my soul sisters who never believed I could do anything less than a thousand times what I thought I could; Josh Cowart and the Ruth's Chris family at Salt Lake City; all my cheer squad on Facebook and through the blog; my friends at SoFi and Geomni for working with my PTO needs and encouraging me all the way; my beta readers, without whom I came across as a rambling dolt; my siblings, in-laws, nieces and nephews, many of whom have loved me and been my cheer squad since before I could even ride; and my parents, Dan and Renee Hawkley. I got my first "road bike" for Christmas in 1980, if I remember the year right. Dad passed in 2004, but I catch glimpses of him on the road when I'm out there, and he has always cheered me on from wherever he is. And Mom, thank you for cheering through the fear that I'm going to get myself killed, and just remember—if I didn't survive it I couldn't have written it, so don't let any of the stories freak you out.

With all my love,

JypsyJill

Glossary of terms particular to this tale:

SomeDay: Days that, unless you actively choose them, never come.

An OtherDay: Days that, unless you actively choose something else, will probably be swallowed up by mundane tasks, anxiety, and depression.

DayMath: SomeDays > OtherDays, AnyDayAlive > AnyDayNot, EveryDayCompleted = SuccessfulDay

Boston Marathon: The Holy Grail of running. You have to run a qualifying marathon within a certain timeframe to even gain entry.

Century Ride: 100 miles. There is also a metric century, which is 100K, or just over 62 miles.

Crazy Patriot's Day: The day the Boston Marathon is run, annually, which is the third Monday in April.

Monday, April 21, 1969: Crazy Patriot's Day, and somewhat coincidentally, the day I was born. I have always considered myself both a Patriot and more than a little bit Crazy.

Anxiety: Anticipating disaster, being overly concerned about money, health, family, work, or other issues, and often being unable to control one's worry about such issues—even with logic and reasoning. Perhaps particularly with logic and reasoning.

All of the All of the: Everything emotional. "All y'all", but for the emotional stuff instead of referring to groups of people.

Pleaser: Someone who craves praise, thrives on positive feedback, and doesn't quite know what to do if they are taken away. Will look for these things sometimes in inappropriate places.

Bulging Disc: The short definition is pain. The long definition is that a disc between vertebrae "bulges" between two vertebrae, often pinching nerves. In the lower back this can lead to muscle weakness, numbness, or tingling in one or both legs, and even in extreme cases, paralysis.

Mic Drop: I suspect it's meant to say, "There is nothing more to say." For me a "mic drop" is the ringing in my ears when someone drops a life-changing bit of news; the feedback of a million neurons trying to process what just happened. If you haven't heard it, go to Open Mic night at a comedy club, Karaoke night at your family reunion, or a wedding where the cousin who volunteered so he'd get an invite is in charge of the sound.

But it's a dry heat: This the small print in Wikipedia when you search for Phoenix, Aridzona. (Shut up, spell-check. That's exactly how Arizona is spelled in my dictionary!)

Climbing: Any time the bike is on an uphill slope, I'm climbing. I have been on 7% grades where I was passing semis at my speed of under 4 mph. If you are able to stand up in the saddle and use all your leg muscles as well as your weight for power during a climb, it is best, but sometimes the climb is too long to allow for a sustained charge up the mountain. While Miley Cyrus wasn't 100% right about it being all about the climb, often climbs are followed by exhilarating speed on the downhill. On this ride I climbed the equivalent of Mount Everest three times.

You Only Die Once

Brazillion: A number so large even the angels stopped counting approximately a million ago—also known as "seventy times seven" in The Bible. Not to be confused with Brazilian, who are the delightful people populating the largest country in South America, or a very painful spa procedure.

Australia: A continent built of the corpses of a quadrillion ants that linked arms during The Great Flood and floated around the world, all the while reproducing and becoming heavier and heavier, until ultimately the ones at the bottom sank to the ocean floor and created a new continent, but it is still entirely made of ants (take a breath!), where my family and I spent 9 months living and working, fighting jet lag, and realizing that bats are the icons of creepiness.

Clips and Shoes: Clips (or clipless) and Shoes help utilize the Push and Pull of the leg muscles by essentially strapping your feet to the sprocket that turns the bike chain. If you're not clipped in on long rides, you're really only using your quads, risking injury, and using more energy than you need to. Plus you don't get the cyclist's calves that are so defined, and if you're going to ride a lot, why not get the legs to show for it?

Tubeless: I cannot stress enough how wonderful tubeless tires are. A tech puts liquid sealant into the tire, and when you inflate (like you do any other tire), the sealant sloshes around inside, sealing any small punctures and the bead line, allowing you to stay on the road. You already have them on your car (have you tried to price inner tubes for your car recently? I don't think you can find them!), and if you are doing hundreds of miles a month on a bike, you owe it to yourself to get this done. You're welcome.

8

Lighthouse: Magical buildings that help people who are lost at sea figure out where they are, give people hope, and, even though it tends to smell of must, mold, and humidity, would be the perfect place in which Burgess Meredith could sit and read in "Time Enough at Last"—a Twilight Zone episode that has messed with my mind since the moment I saw it when it was rerun probably 40 years ago.

November 20: The day my dad died in 2004, also coincidentally the day in 1959 that "Time Enough at Last" first aired on television.

SAG: Support and Gear, the vehicle that transports it, and the driver of said vehicle 99% of the time this was my husband, Randy, who not only transported everything, but also prepared anything and waited for hours alongside the road. Among the services a SAG car provides, in this case: peanut butter and jelly sandwiches, instant oatmeal mixed with applesauce, Slim Jims, water, ice, sunscreen, bug spray, getting my head on straight, candy, protein powder, BCAA+ mix that tastes like poison and looks like antifreeze (who thought buying sour gummy candy flavor was a good idea? Wait, that was me...), foot and back rubs, making sure tires are inflated, lubing the chain, and following me on dark roads during midnight rides during the heat of summer. Oh, and driving while I slept, paying for 98% or so of everything, and making sure I was happy and healthy along the way. I am nowhere without the SAG.

Cowards die many times before their deaths;

The valiant never taste of death but once.

-William Shakespeare, *Julius Caesar* Act One, Scene Two

CHAPTER 13
FEAR

If you got this book because you know me, you are likely familiar with my struggle with anxiety and depression. If you do not know me, I trust you will believe that I have suffered through varying degrees of anxiety and depression for many years—since long before my children were born—but heightened by stress and hitting an apex upon my father's sudden death in 2004. I have posted detailed explanations on Facebook about what my panic attacks have felt like, as well as crippling days of depression where I could hardly get out of bed. Everything hurt, yes, but everything hurt because my mind was so deep in an abyss that I couldn't see light, and struggling to come up from that emotional depth gave me The Bends[1].

---

[1] The Bends: also known as Decompression Sickness; is typically caused by surfacing too quickly after a deep dive, when nitrogen bubbles form in the bloodstream. The condition can cause rashes, joint pain, headaches, and paralysis.

I've considered for quite some time how much I should share about where I think the anxiety and depression came from. I certainly don't want it to feel to anybody like I'm placing blame, or like I was a victim of the circumstances of a crummy childhood. I am not, and I was not. I have a fantastic life. I know that, and knowing that I have nothing to complain about makes it feel much worse. *I* am the person saying, "Snap out of it! . . . You've got so much to live for! . . . You could fix this if you really tried. . . . Ugh. This again? Aren't you tired of this yet? . . . Are you sure you're not just feeling this way because you're bored, or want attention, or are upset about something?" Perhaps knowing where and how my seeds of anxiety were planted will help you understand where I'm coming from.

According to my mother, Renee Hawkley, I taught myself to read when I was three and a half. I was always precocious and a people pleaser. I had a pair of shared imaginary friends with my older brother Danny (shout out to Frank and Rayna, wherever you are!), and we loved to play outside with them, sharing many adventures in the early 1970s. Life was good, easy, and happy. One day in the summer after I turned four, my family cooked dinner on a Hibachi grill and my dad dumped the spent charcoal at the edge of the garden next to the sandbox so it could cool down before spreading it in the garden to augment the soil.

The next morning I wanted to go swimming (i.e.: splashing. I was, after all, only four), and Mom, who was pregnant at the time, needed to buy a little time before taking us to the pool, so she challenged me to do several good deeds before she would take us to the pool. So I went about looking for places I could "do good." I made my bed. I picked up my brother's toy. I brushed the dog. I went outside to see if there was anything I could do out there, and saw what I believed was a pile of sand in the corner of the garden.

Dad had scolded Danny and me more than once about sand in the garden. It all felt like dirt to me, but I knew that sand in the garden was a bad thing for whatever reason, so I decided the sand needed to go back into the sand box. I reached both hands in and closed them tightly around the soft, greyish-white . . . charcoal. Realizing it was a huge mistake, but not being able to connect the searing pain with anything I understood, I pulled out my hands and ran toward the house screaming. Instinct dictated that I shake my hands, trying to get the pain off. With each flick of my hands, chunks of blackened skin flew off, and in my naïveté I thought that they were bees stinging me over and over again. The layers of skin that weren't melting off were a mass of blisters on top of blisters, which were popping and dripping water down my arms. Remember the scene from *Raiders of the Lost Ark* when the Nazi guy's face melts off when they open the Ark of the Covenant? That, but with my hands, and the burns didn't go all the way to the bone like they did with the guy's skull.

I had tried to do a good thing. I learned at four years old that sometimes doing good things will turn on you. I am very fortunate that quick thinking on my mother's part and a good doctor made for no visible scars, but the scars on my psyche have lasted my entire life.

I spent the next six weeks with my hands bound together, slathered in a healing salve, fingers as tight in fists as I could get them, in order to make sure that the knuckle folds didn't heal flat and make them unable to bend. My husband Randy and I were chatting about random things recently and comparing finger bending. (I did say random, didn't I?) I had never felt like I had any lasting damage—other than one spot on my pointer finger where my fingerprint doesn't line up—but suffice it to say, my fingers don't bend nearly as much as his do. The end joint of every one of my fingers only bends to about 45 degrees, even if I press on the joint with the other hand.

Read that paragraph's opening sentence again. I spent the next six weeks with my hands *bound together*. I was a four-year-old who could read on her own, but physically I was an infant. I couldn't feed myself. I couldn't wipe myself. I couldn't wear any clothes that had sleeves, so mom ended up making me several jumpers that crossed in the back and buttoned at the shoulder so I could have something to wear on my torso. (Gratefully, they were in style at the time.) I couldn't blow my nose or pick up a toy or turn a page without help. Oh, and mom was pregnant with her fourth, had a one-year-old toddling around at the same time, and a husband who worked long hours. Her frustration with her situation was palpable, even for a four-year-old. When I became a mom myself I understood a lot better, but four-year-old Jill just wanted Mom to be happy and pleased with me, and due to my inability to fend for myself, it felt like she was angry at me when she had to feed me and the baby, turn the page in my book, or place a baby doll in my arms so I could rock it to sleep in my miniature rocking chair.

By the time I was physically healed from that disaster we had moved back to Orem, Utah for my dad to go to law school, and I was six years old. That summer we went to a parade in downtown Provo, the neighboring town. After the parade was over, Danny and I were teasing each other and messing around, and either Dad or Mom suggested we race to the car. Again, this was the mid-1970s. There weren't as many abductions, murders, or molestations in the news at the time (though many were actually happening), and Provo felt pretty safe. Don't judge my parents. They are and were amazing. So we raced to the car, but he was faster than I was, and either he turned and I didn't or I turned and he didn't, but when I got to where I thought the car was, neither the car nor my brother were there. I wandered around for a few minutes, and little to nothing looked familiar except Mount Timpanogos, which I could see from my front window at home, from the playground at school, from the church parking lot, and from where I was standing in downtown Provo.

That enormous Rocky Mountain was comforting and gave me confidence. I was smart. I could figure out how to get home: just walk the direction we came from and get to the main road. It had felt like there hadn't been many turns. Easy peasy! So I walked two blocks south to Center Street, turned west, and walked several more blocks, the whole while just *knowing* that I could find my way home, and oddly comforted by the traffic passing me as other parade goers made their way home, thinking that perhaps my family would be among them and pick me up, cutting my walk short.

Forty-five minutes or so later (estimated, since it is roughly 1.75 miles and my legs were short) when I got to the freeway sign that reads "Salt Lake City" and points north, and "Las Vegas" and points south, I knew I didn't want either of them, and I got scared. This was the road we had come in on, after all, and I didn't know which way I was supposed to go. There was also a "No Pedestrians" sign. If I had known that walking north on University would have gotten me into "the grid[2]" of Orem, I would have done that, but I didn't really understand the grid yet. I had long been told to be wary of strangers, especially strangers who knew I was lost; so when tears came unbidden to my eyes, I got even more afraid. Strangers could kidnap you if you were lost, and nobody would know where to look for you. So when the woman at the house on the corner saw me crying and asked if I was lost, I told her no, I knew exactly where I was, I just didn't know how to get *home* from where I absolutely knew I was. She was kind and sweet and sensed my fear, but she was also on her way out the door for a family event, so instead of taking me home, she called the police.

My first (and hopefully only) ride in the back of a police car was terrifying. I believed I was in deep trouble, since only bad people rode in police cars. So when the police officer tried to make it a fun adventure for me by turning on the lights and

---

[2] Utah's road system is set up on a grid, with a central reference point as the center X/Y axis. The blocks count up or down from the center axis, and if you know how it works, you can generally find your way to whatever coordinates you are given as an address. For example, 200 N 500 W would be two blocks north from the center point and five blocks west.

sirens, I not only felt like I had done something *terribly* wrong, I also was hugely embarrassed. When we got to the police station a few minutes later, they put me in a room with a television playing game shows and brought me popsicles and ice cream and candy bars and orange soda and a teddy bear, and all the stuff my parents wouldn't let me have at the parade because then they would have had to buy four of them, and price gouging has always been a thing. The police were impressed that I could read on my own and knew my full address and telephone number, and they had a female officer come listen to me read over the top of Bob Barker and *The Price is Right*. She was really nice and prettier, I thought, than Police Woman on TV (played by Angie Dickinson) which I wasn't allowed to watch, but had seen promos for.

What felt like an eternity later (but was probably closer to forty-five minutes), I looked up and saw my somewhat panicked dad looking through the narrow window into the room. The police had called the house until finally someone answered, and Dad had rushed back to Provo to come claim me. Remember, this was the '70s. They didn't have 911 emergency services, Amber alerts, or cell phones. My parents had one car at the time, and four kids under seven years old. While I am certain the police didn't judge my parents for going home, (after all, what else could they do at the time?) and it's not like I got into actual *trouble* for getting lost, I felt even more awful when I got home. Mom had been crying, and I could see it. She was so afraid of what might have happened that she barely spoke to me for hours that felt like months, just hugging me and crying some more. I vowed then and there in my sweet baby angel's heart of hearts to never make her *nearly* that angry, never, ever again, as long as I live. (Sorry, mom. I know I dropped the ball on that vow about a brazillion[3] times over the past 44 years, despite my vow. Read the last part of the dedication again, please.)

The point is this: I came by my anxiety and depression due to my circumstances, but I am not a victim of them. I wasn't abused. I wasn't unwanted and didn't come from a broken family or pitiable circumstances. My family loved me. We had our issues and spats, but what healthy family in the real world doesn't? Four-year-old me didn't want to have my mom put me on the toilet and wipe my bum when I was done emptying my bladder, but the fact is I *did* have to. Six-year-old me thought my mom, who was practically paralyzed with fear over what might have happened to her then-only daughter, was so *angry* at me that she wasn't going to speak to me ever, ever again; that I'd done something *so wrong* by getting lost, and then telling a *stranger* I was lost, and (gasp!) *having to ride in the back of a police car*! *At six*! From my view Dad had saved me, and would do so many times over the next not-quite-30 years. Every time Dad "saved" me, it was because I had made a simple mistake, did not have the knowledge or judgment I needed to make a good decision, or found myself in over my head.

---

[3] A number so large even the angels stopped counting approximately a million ago - also known as "seventy times seven" in The Bible. Not to be confused with Brazilian, who are the delightful people populating the largest country in South America, or a very painful spa procedure.

I wish I (or *someone*) had known my six-year-old or four-year-old self well enough to sit her down and say, "Look. This isn't your fault. You're not stupid for getting hurt. You're not dumb because you made a mistake. You're not bad because you needed help. You aren't being punished for making a mistake, or humiliated because you are worthless. You feel pain because you got hurt. You feel sad because you miss being somewhat independent. Soon you'll be freed from your bandages and your hands won't hurt so much, and you'll be able to feed yourself and wash yourself and you won't need so much help. Nothing horrifying happened when you were lost. You don't have to be afraid of the world."

I wish I'd had the maturity and understanding that *all* the experiences would be for my good. I'm 50 and I'm not quite sure I believe that yet, even though I remind myself every day that it is true. Maybe I wouldn't have believed them even if they had said it all those years ago. I needed to go through "all of the all of the"[4] to get here, and maybe to get *there*—wherever that is. I do know one thing: I still am a pleaser[5]. I always want people to like me, though I have gotten much better about deciding that if they don't, I don't get to change who I am in order to make them like me.

There's a popular meme that says, "You cannot make everyone happy. You are not a taco." I recognize that I'm not

---

[4] Everything emotional. "All y'all," but for the emotional stuff instead of referring to groups of people.

[5] Someone who craves praise, thrives on positive feedback, and doesn't quite know what to do if they are taken away. Will look for these things sometimes in inappropriate places.

for everyone. I have shocking news for you: even tacos aren't everybody's thing (I know, blasphemy, right?). I can be more than people want to try and deal with. But I also recognize that I am worthy of their love, even if I never perceive that I have received it. Nothing I do, say, or believe can discount my worth. It was determined long before I conceived of a cross country ride, long before I ever doubted it, long before I caught a glimpse of it with a sideways glance at my reflection in a store window and thought, "I wanna be like her Someday[6]."

Someday I hope that I will be fully healed of anxiety and depression[7]. Forty-six years of highly focused, subconscious practice at something makes for an extremely difficult habit to break, but I have hope that I will at least be managing it instead of it managing me. I was diagnosed with PTSD in January 2019, and that is a whole 'nother ball of wax that at least explains why I started down the anxiety path as young as four, but I am doing better post-diagnosis, since at least how I'm feeling makes a little more sense and I understand why I am triggered.

But here's the thing: I'm not going to paint the most flattering picture of either the coast-to-coast ride or the lessons I learned along the way just because it makes for a great story. I'll tell you the heartbreaking and thrilling details as best as I remember them, and I will try to keep the drama of my emotions to a dull roar. Please know that I tell it how I

---

[6] A day that, unless you actively choose it, never comes.

[7] Somedays > Other Days, Any Day Alive > Any Day Not, Every Day Completed = Successful Day. Otherwise referred to as Day Math.

experienced it, and that I don't mean to exaggerate for effect. Also please know that the triumphs I discuss are, at least for me, huge. I did not make or break any land speed records. Guinness doesn't care about my accomplishment; but this is *my* book, not theirs. They write the biggest, fastest, smallest, largest, slowest, oldest, youngest, most, and least they can find in the world. In my book you will read the biggest, fastest, smallest, largest, slowest, oldest, youngest, most, and least as a bit of a peek into *my* world. I do not wish to glorify or glamorize myself or my issues, nor to give them any more voice than they need. I hope that if you, my friend, are able to relate to any of the situations that come up in this book, that you will feel that we have a kinship. But please also know that I no longer *suffer from* anxiety and depression. I am *thriving despite* anxiety and depression.

∴∴∴

I met my current doctor in November 2018. At my last checkup she said, "I would not recognize the you I met just nine months ago if I saw her on the street, you have changed so much." It is true that physically I am much the same. My labs are likely similar, if not identical. But I am a totally different person than the fearful person I was, even since I first met her. And it is likely due to the fact that on her insistence I saw a psychologist, which visits I will discuss in a later chapter. Suffice it to say for now that while my life is far from perfect, and I do not take my current mental stability for granted by any stretch, I am able to see more clearly the way forward, and know what to do when the big storms do hit, as I am constantly reminded that they will.

Elizabeth Gilbert, in her book *Big Magic*, addresses her fear, calling it by name, and does it without spite, anger, or any noticeable negative emotion, saying this:

> Dearest Fear: Creativity and I are about to go on a road trip together. I understand you'll be joining us, because you always do. I acknowledge that you believe you have an important job to do in my life, and that you take your job seriously. Apparently your job is to induce complete panic whenever I'm about to do anything interesting—and, may I say, you are superb at your job. So by all means, keep doing your job, if you feel you must. But I will also be doing my job on this road trip, which is to work hard and stay focused. And Creativity will be doing its job, which is to remain stimulating and inspiring.
>
> There's plenty of room in this vehicle for all of us, so make yourself at home, but understand this: Creativity and I are the only ones who will be making any decisions along the way. I recognize and respect that you are part of this family, and so I will never exclude you from our activities, but still—your suggestions will never be followed. You're allowed to have a seat, and you're allowed to have a voice, but you are not allowed to have a vote. You're not allowed to touch the road maps; you're not allowed to suggest detours; you're not allowed to fiddle with the temperature. Dude, you're not even allowed to touch the radio. But above all else, my

dear old familiar friend, you are absolutely forbidden to drive.[8]

Fear was the backseat driver for much of my life. It had veto power over every vote, silently manipulating every turn with impeccable logic and guilt, all in the name of protecting me. On occasion I would make commitments or arrangements that bypassed fear while it was asleep, curled up behind me with headphones on drowning out the sound of the road. Always I would pay for those decisions with a backlash of fear, and if they didn't pan out, fear would sit in the background saying, "You knew I didn't want to do that, and you did it anyway. You see why I never let you do anything? You're a fool for not listening to me." And I got a little bit smaller and it got a little bit bigger.

More on that in Chapter 4. I'm not going to delve much deeper for the moment, because that's not how the ride played out.

---

[8] Elizabeth Gilbert, *Big Magic: Creative Living Beyond Fear* (Riverhead Books, 2016), p.22

It is the same with people as it is with riding a bike. Only when moving can one comfortably maintain one's balance.

-Albert Einstein, Physicist, in a letter to his son, Eduard, Feb 5, 1930

CHAPTER 12
"HOW *FAR*?"

In 1994 Oprah Winfrey ran the Marine Corps marathon in 4:29:20, shortly after she turned 40. My daughter had been born just a few months prior, and I was forty-five pounds overweight, feeling overwhelmed, and sad. An hour before Oprah's "I ran a marathon!" show, I pushed Rachel in the stroller two blocks to the convenience store and bought, with two dollars I had found in the laundry, the biggest Slurpee they had and a king-sized Reese's. I watched the show in my downstairs apartment while downing a grand total of roughly 900 calories, which consists of roughly 125 grams of sugar, (just over ½ cup) crying and bemoaning my fate. But hey, if Oprah could do it, why couldn't I? She had a trainer, sure. But that didn't mean she was better than I was. It just meant I needed to find something that motivated and drove me to want to keep going. "But... who am I kidding?", I asked myself, "I can't do what she did. She has all the time in the world, no kids, and I have this baby. I'll do that in a few years when the baby is older."

In 1997 I had d'Artagnan, and the struggle with weight and self-esteem continued. By this time we had moved out of the downstairs apartment and into our own home—and the convenience store was four blocks away. I was going to do this weight-loss thing the right way. I decided to walk every day to the convenience store. I also cut back on my slurpee size to a 32 oz. and got the more sensible king-sized Kit Kat, dropping my daily "splurge" calories to a mere 600 with 116 grams of sugar (just under 1/2 cup). But I was walking twice as far! How could I still be gaining weight??? Lol.

By October 2002 I had hit my breaking point. My "baby" entered kindergarten and I hadn't lost an ounce—far from it. I had gained more than forty-five pounds post-delivery. In fairness, that's "only" nine pounds a year for five years. That isn't "end of the world" weight, is it? I wasn't as heavy as I could be…

Randy and I went to Las Vegas for a weekend business trip, and I walked more the first day than I probably had done in the previous five years combined. We got back to the resort late that evening, and I was sitting next to the pool with Randy's coworker, Dawn Ralston. I remember getting emotional as I felt my heart racing and unable to catch my breath. I was sure I was having a heart attack, and I had left my 8-year-old and 5-year-old at home in Midvale, Utah and they would never understand why I died. I took my pulse. Ultimately it was just a panic attack, but for me it was a wake-up call. The following

Wednesday I was at Weight Watchers with Dawn, and we were on our way to a healthier lifestyle.

In April, 2004 I ran my first ever 5K. In May I hit my goal weight, a total of seventy-five pounds lower than my heaviest, and I was running almost every day. I started working as a reading aid and playground monitor for the kids' school part-time in the fall, and enjoyed that as well. I was on top of the world as I envisioned running my first marathon in April 2005. I'd signed up with a training group that raised money for the Huntsman Cancer Center, and the first training run would happen November 20, 2004.

If that date sounds familiar, it's because that is the day my father died. My alarm was set for 5:00 AM, and I had my running shoes and tights set out, all ready to go. The phone rang at 4:12 AM. My youngest brother Ethan dropped the news, and my life was forever changed.

I called the coach at 5:30 to tell her I wouldn't make it that week or likely the next, but that she could plan on me the following week, but thankfully she wasn't there—I didn't want to talk to someone I didn't really even know and tell her what was going on. It felt like it wasn't even "real" until I told someone. I left a message on her voicemail and hastily packed clothes and random items for an unexpected trip to Boise. Because my running clothes and shoes were already out, I threw them in my bag. I ended up using them several times over the next several days as I tried to process my grief in the city that overnight had become the place I hated most in this world. It took my father away from me. For the first time in my memory,

I couldn't feel the fear that had been present since I was four. All I felt was emptiness, loneliness, and anger.

The funeral was a blur of people I couldn't see through my tears, and the sound of my heartbeat was louder than anything else, all of which seemed muffled and distant. None of it made sense without dad—like trying to duct tape a sympathy card to the Titanic on its way to the bottom of the ocean—but it also didn't make sense if he had been there, so I was in a paradox of pain.

When we got home, I wanted everything to be "normal" again. I ran a lot, and got back to marathon training, and successfully ran my first marathon, as planned, in April 2005, but I was far from "normal." I decided that running a single marathon the same month as my birthday was cool, but wouldn't it be cool if I could run the Boston marathon? So I looked up when Boston was run. Turns out, as you read in the glossary, the Boston marathon is run on the third Monday in April, every year, which meant it would be run on my 39th birthday, 2008. Going from complete couch potato to running a marathon in three years isn't too much training to qualify, even though I had to cut more than two hours off my first marathon attempt, and maybe if a miracle happened, I could get qualified. If it's run on your birthday, you should make it a priority to run it, right?

I ran a couple of half-marathons and 10Ks and even a few Sprint triathlons (though I don't know many people who actually sprint 500 meters of swimming, 12 miles of cycling, and 3.12 miles of running in a row) as well as the Saint George Marathon in Saint George, Utah in October of 2006, but I didn't get qualified at Saint George for Boston. I still needed to cut more than 90 minutes from my time, so I was training as often as I could— riding a bike to the gym and back, lifting weights for up to two hours a day, and running every morning for at least an hour. My fastest mile was just under eight minutes, and I needed to average 8:12 per mile for 26.2 miles to qualify.

About eight months after Dad died we moved to southern California, where I enjoyed training year-round in the amazing weather of Orange County. Early in the Spring of 2007 I was planting some flowers in my flower boxes on the front deck, when I suddenly felt a searing pain shooting from my lower back to my left ankle. It was so severe that for a moment I thought I'd been stabbed in the back. I was on my hands and knees, and couldn't stand up on my own, but since d'Artagnan (ten years old at the time) was helping, he was able to run inside and get the phone so I could call Randy at the office.

I was at a local chiropractor's office within an hour, where it was determined that I was suffering from a bulging disc in my lower back. When he said, "There is no way on earth you're coming back from this to run Boston in fifteen months," I took a deep, tentative breath and asked, "Okay, so can I do it by April 2009?", unable to fathom that he could say anything worse. "We can get you back to long-distance running," he said, "but eventually it will destroy the nerves going from your back to your legs and you will likely be in a wheelchair by the time you are sixty."

Mic drop.

I remember feeling tiny, weak, and broken when the small piece of me that didn't want to give up asked, "Well, when will I be in a wheelchair if I do stop long-distance running?" (as if being in a wheelchair at sixty would be okay if I was going to be in a wheelchair by sixty-five anyway? Lol).

"You'll walk until you're dead."

Then the discussion began about what I can do after my disc issues were fixed. Weight lifting was fine (ironically, I thought). Walking was great. Riding a bike would be a great way to get the aerobic exercise I craved. I latched on to that thought. "Okay, but how far can I ride a bike?"

"Go as far as you want to go."

Challenge accepted.

In October 2007 I rode my first 50+ mile (52 miles) ride in the desert ~100 miles east of San Diego with my neighbor Mike Silverberg. It was an early start that morning, but looked to be a decent ride, until the Santa Ana winds kicked in and provided an intense headwind during the last 17 miles of the ride. Unbeknownst to us at the time, a pole holding a power transformer in the San Diego area had been knocked over by the force of those exact winds and sparked what ended up being the second-largest wildfire in the state until that time. (It was knocked down to third in 2018.) It was wicked hot, and I thought at the end, "I am never doing anything that crazy again."

Nothing compares to the simple pleasure of riding a bike.

-John F. Kennedy

CHAPTER 11
JET LAG + AUSTRALIAN TV
=
"YOU KNOW WHAT WOULD BE COOL...?"

Following the global economic crisis and company-wide layoffs of more than 1,000 people at Randy's work, my family and I moved in September 2009 to the Gold Coast of Australia, and I had a wicked case of jet lag for about a month after we arrived. Early one morning I was watching an Aussie news report about 35-year-old Dave Alley, who was planning a ride around the continent of Australia. He wouldn't be the first person to have done it, but his goal was to do it faster than anyone ever had. To be honest, I don't remember the news piece I saw very well, but with a little bit of searching to remind myself what his actual goal was, found a news piece written after he completed his record-breaking ride on November 3, 2011; in 37 days. From the article by Amy Simmons: (full article can be found at https://www.abc.net.au/news/2011-11-04/man-cycles-round-australia-in-record-time/3626614)

DAD CYCLES AROUND AUSTRALIA
IN RECORD 37 DAYS

Mr Alley says while the race itself took just under 38 days, the entire challenge was a two-year process.

"Training-wise it consisted of anywhere from 20 hours-plus a week of actual cycling, but it was probably more like 40 hours a week in total—so it was really another full-time job. I had two physio sessions a week, a chiropractic session a week, and we were also using float tanks for the recovery process," he said.

Mr Alley says he had two key motivations—wanting to achieve something significant before the age of 40, and his children.

"I have three kids now but I had twins five years ago that were born three months prematurely," he said.

"When they were born it was a real battle, they were in intensive care for three months and it was touch and go at times whether they'd actually make it, but they pulled through and have got no ongoing health issues at all."

He says at that point he took on an ironman triathlon to raise money for the twins' hospital.

"I was never good at endurance sport, so it became a challenge to take something on in that field," Mr Alley explained.

"I was so inspired and motivated by what the kids had been through and their struggle for life and that really inspired me to continue on this career path and take on another adventure."

When I saw that, I remember thinking, "Man, that guy is *nuts!* Even if he *can* do something significant by the time he's 40, Australia is *huge!*"

I had already turned 40 earlier that spring, and although I had completed marathons, my dream of Boston was long since dashed. In the dark of my quiet apartment at 4AM I secretly envied him and his goal while cheering him on in my heart. Sometime in the night, before I finally either fell asleep or gave up and went for a walk on the beach, my somewhat addled brain flashed the idea, "You know what would be cool? Doing something that yes, others have done, but that *not* everybody has done—on a bike—but nothing nearly as crazy as that guy. That guy is insane..."

A seed was planted.

By June of 2010 we had moved back to Sandy, Utah and one of the first things we bought (having sold everything before we left for Australia) was a decent road bike the salesman recommended for cross-country use— a Trek aluminum road bike with the carbon fork—with clips and shoes (which I had never used). The seedling had popped through the soil and begun to look like something that resembled the possibility of a plant. Which is to say, neon yellow-green, weak, and likely to drop dead at the first sign of trouble.

I tried riding with clips three or four times, but found that every time I got on the bike I got more and more afraid of what would happen when I had to stop, and ended up avoiding riding. Clips basically tie your feet to the pedals, which are smaller than regular pedals, and most people who have just begun riding with them fall a lot, due to the lack of practice twisting your foot out of the clipped position before coming to a complete stop, but the wonderful thing is that they also allow you to use *all* the muscles in the legs, which is much more efficient as well as preventing stress injuries. Be that as it may, I put fewer than 100 miles on my schmancy bike the first year I owned it because I was so afraid of looking foolish when I fell over at stop signs and stop lights.

The next spring, I changed back to traditional pedals. No sense spending almost $1,000 on a bicycle I wasn't going to ride. Two years later in the Spring of 2013 I was challenged by a friend with a mutual love of the bike to participate in a century ride, and I said, "Yeah, maybe Someday", (there's that "Someday" again. DayMath) but she got into my head, and I wondered if I could train enough to get it done by the fall. I looked up century rides in my area, and there was a women-only ride on Saturday, September 14, which happens to be my dad's birthday. Before I really knew what was going on, I was signed up and planning how I could achieve it. I trained, and I trained hard, and on September 14, I did it. I couldn't express until sometime Sunday afternoon what I had felt.

From my Facebook note September 15, 2013:

IT'S A MIRACLE!
September 15, 2013 at 10:23 PM
It's a Miracle!
First of all, I have the most amazing husband ever. He started as support crew for one, and ended up personal support crew for 5. All the girls were jealous, and it was magical to see him speed up a street where someone had a flat tire, grab the pump, and start pumping. I was terrified of the cattle guards and a couple of stretches of dirt road—and even though the rain had pretty well packed the dirt road sections down, he parked at the

far side of them and waited for us to get past before leapfrogging to the next bad stretch to make sure if I did fall, he'd be able to help as soon as possible. When he started getting pummeled with rain, he came looking for our make-shift team (made on the road) who had all thrown our jackets in the car. He didn't find us; we were ahead of him, and not even touched by the storm.

Shortly after lunch, we were headed up the road and wanted different music. He turned up his radio and blasted AC/DC so we could all hear. We laughed and sang, and rode. The only place I walked the bike was over the first cattle guard. I did not fall once.

When learning how to "small talk", they say to talk about the weather. This was no small thing yesterday. I couldn't have asked for a more perfect day... for me. Other girls were not so blessed. When we were driving to Payson, I could see the stars. We got there and I was pointing out Orion's belt and Cassiopeia. It was chilly, but not brisk, and there was no wind. An hour later, the whole sky was overcast as we started, which made it nice and cool, but they weren't rain clouds, so we were riding with a lovely parasol and a fantastic background for the color of the trees and the mountains to "pop" against. Usually blue skies take some of that away, but the grey accentuated it. I'd done the first 50 before, a few weeks back, and had hot, blue skies the whole way. I'll take grey every day of the week. The thin cloud cover started to dissipate as I hit mile 30, and I had about 40 minutes of blue skies and a few puffy clouds as I made a new friend (who I'll talk about in a bit) and we pushed our bikes to the next aid station. I even got a little sun during that, but not as much as to burn; just a little color.

We hung out at the aid station for a little while and caught our breath and took our jackets off, and then rode toward the canyon. And though the road into the canyon is a gradual uphill, we were going pretty quickly as we got into it. I was a little surprised, as when I rode this part before, I was trudging up this part. The canyon is a narrow, two-lane road with great turns, and it is almost all downhill. As I was flying down these turns, I looked to my left, and there was the most enormous black cloud against an otherwise blue sky. All I could think was, we have to get out of this canyon before that starts to dump. It's going to be ugly for whoever gets caught in that! But the little band of sisters was a little bit behind me, so I didn't point it out, and just pressed on.

We made it out of the canyon without a drop of rain hitting us, and two miles later were eating lunch. Girls who got there 10 minutes after we did were talking about how bad it was; the rain apparently started as cups of water, and then it turned into buckets, and then just a WALL of water just hit them in the face. There were reports of hail. There were women who were soaked to the skin sitting next to women who were completely dry at lunch.

As the ride progressed, we had alternating grey skies and blue. It was amazing. Several times I thought, there's no possible way we're getting past THAT cloud before it dumps. And then it didn't. At one point Kristin said, "I don't think were' getting out of this without getting soaked." And I looked at the clouds and said, "Check this out. The raining one is north of us, and we're heading straight into the break between it and the REALLY big one. I think we can make it, and just go behind it!" I don't know that even I believed it, but it kept us going. The girls 3 minutes behind us (so roughly ¾ of a mile) were forced by the support car to turn back as they got hit by hail and hurricane force gusts of wind. Not that we didn't get wind, but we had ZERO rain.

We turned north again at the top of a small slope that we had to BATTLE to get up because of wind gusts. And were right behind the big cloud I'd pointed out to Kristin. And we kept going. When we hit the road we'd been on before and it was totally dry the first time, our tires were throwing water up on us. It was soaked. It LOOKED like a totally different road.

There had been a guy out doing woodworking on his front porch, and all his equipment was still out there, but the wood was drenched. There was a field with about two inches of standing water covering it that had been completely dry on our first pass. Where there had been men working ncxt to a ditch, there were yard tools abandoned as they took cover. And yet there was nothing coming down on us.

At the last aid station (with 5 miles to go) we just pressed on. There had been a support truck following us for approximately 15 miles. In the last three miles it started to sprinkle. I would guess I got hit by 100 very small rain drops in those last three miles. Almost a gift of, "you did great, cool off a little…" for the end.

I'd trained alone. I was ready. I knew I was. And I totally could have done it on my own, I believe. But. About 25 miles in, a lady came up behind me and we started talking. I was listening to music (thank goodness for Spotify Premium... I would have lost my mind without it!) and she mentioned that it was awesome that I had music. There was a water only aid station just beyond where we met, and I gave her one of my honey waffles ... I had in my little pouch, because it was another 12 miles until there was an aid station with any kind of nourishment or even electrolytes. We rode together while she "waited" for some of the rest of the girls she was riding with; Jyll, Jane, & Patti.

We of course got to talking. It is, after all, ME we're talking about. And we talked about Randy and how we'd met, and my dad, and lots of chit chat as we pedaled. We were pretty much best friends by the time we got to the next aid station. Randy drove past and took pictures just as I finished the story about how we'd met. That was fun. We took a break and took off the warm jackets (wind-breakers, mostly, but some of the other girls on our now TEAM had extra pants on) and put them in our car instead of sending them on with the support vehicles to be picked up at the end.

When we left that aid station, we headed north into Goshen Canyon. It wasn't hot, but it was nice, and we didn't need those jackets at that point. Between the five of us we spent several miles talking and chatting about music, friends, church, life, work, and love. The miles melted away and it was easy. Just a fun little bike ride with a group of really fun ladies—all with different interests and backgrounds, but who shared a lot in common as well. The road leading into Goshen Canyon is a slight uphill slope, but it wasn't hard. We passed several girls along the way, and I told them about the cattle guards in canyon.

The cattle guards scared me to death. They are metal grates over about a foot deep gully in the road. There is a roughly 6 inch gap between the metal. If you hit them wrong, your tire will stop and you'll go flying. I ALWAYS walk over cattle guards. And the first one, I did, and told the girls I'd catch up. Something about watching them all go over them without stopping—just slowing down so that they had control—gave me confidence, and I crossed the remaining 3 cattle guards along the path with no issues.

The canyon was incredible. We sang, laughed, and kept on pedaling, encouraging each other all the way—any time we needed it. And reminding each other to keep our shoulders back and down. (It's easy, on a road bike, to slouch as the back gets tired—and the best way to combat the fatigue of long rides is to drop the shoulders and pull them back. It's like magic, if you can remember to do it.) Anyway, the 75 miles after meeting Kristin were a gift beyond my wildest imaginations. Yes, the ride was tough. We hit stretches where I thought the wind would flip us over backward. But it was tons easier because I had a team. Get you a team, I believe you can do anything, even in an individual sport.

About three miles from the end, Kristin pulled ahead of me. I was by this point getting pretty fatigued, and at first I thought to catch up with her, but then reminded myself that this—THIS—was MY RIDE. Not Kristin's. She'd been there for the majority of it, and I needed to finish it on my own. The other girls in the team had slowed substantially, and I had one final short climb to get to the park where the finish was.

Randy followed me for a little bit of it, and I couldn't really even look at him for part of it. All I could focus on was keeping my legs moving. The sprinkling hit and felt wonderful. Randy left me right about when I got into the city limits again, as it's a little precarious to be driving as slow as he had to in order to be right next to me once there are cars on the road, but I knew that he was at the finish waiting for me. I got into town and put my head down and pushed up the hill. My legs were so tired. I passed several women who were walking up that hill. I thought to join them, but decided that I had two more rotations in me, and THEN I would join them. Two turned into two more, and two more after that. I had to be looking down, because if I looked at the top of the hill, I would never make it.

It felt like an eternal hill, and at the top was a short flat, and then the park. I took that hill 5 feet at a time, in the easiest gear I have. And got to the flat. I could see Randy at the edge of the park. I could see the "FINISH" banner. For a moment I thought I was just going to pass out before I ever crossed it, but then I just got a rush of adrenaline and shifted gears and finished strong. It wasn't the fastest I'd ridden all day, for sure. But I did finish strong. Kristin was screaming my name at the finish line. I think I caught Randy off guard with the surge of energy, because he hadn't caught up to me to take a picture at the end—but that's okay. I won't forget it.

I talked to Kristin this evening (the day after the ride) and she said she thought I needed to finish on my own. I thanked her for it—and had known that I did need to. Kristin and I will do many rides together, I suspect. (We're already planning another one—just a training ride, don't get crazy...) This one I needed to finish on my own. But I will be forever grateful for the beautiful girl whose infectious smile and encouragement made my ride so fun. Yes, we were meant to be friends. And "hay!!!" it's not like we're made of sugar. I'll leave the ultimate determination of what we ARE made of for another ride. ☺

Finally, I need to thank the rest of my "team." I somehow (though I'd disabled all notifications to my phone) got encouraging words from so many people on Facebook—I didn't think I'd need them, but I did. They mostly came during those first 25 miles when I was "alone" on the road. (with about 300 strangers, but I was riding by myself, for the most part) While I was training, I had multiple people send encouraging texts and emails and personal messages on here that I will never forget—and have printed several for future consumption. I could not have done it without my team of cheerleaders, and the support of countless (and some of them nameless—thank you, Saratoga Springs, Lehi, Eagle Mountain, and Elberta police departments!) people who not only watched my progress via Facebook, but many who sent those encouraging words right when I needed them and many who just said they were thinking about me and wondering how I was doing. I'm not always able to stay safe or able to continue with my planned ride and need "saving."

Sometimes that's at times that Randy can't be there, and I've had to rely on friends to do it. They don't hesitate. They drop everything and come. You know who you are. Thank you.

And those who I haven't called—you were next, I assure you. I know if you're able you'd do it in a heartbeat. I have the most amazing group of friends in the world. I know this is true. Thank you for your encouragement, your support, your belief in me, and your love. You are my team, and I have been honored to have you along for the ride.

All my love,
Jill

Successfully completing 100 miles fueled my desire to cross the country.

That said, it's fun to dream about something like this. Super fun to plan, and scheme and figure out the logistics in a spreadsheet and on paper and using Google Maps to figure out the best route (California to Maine? Washington to Maine? California to South Carolina? Alaska to… no way. Not going to do it) and give it creative and clever names (Lighthouse to Lighthouse? West to West? C-to-C Cycling Factory: Everybody Bike Now?) If I were able to calculate how many hours I spent planning the ride, I'm guessing it would total more than the amount of time I spent on the bicycle, both training and on the route. I worked and reworked and schemed and planned and talked about it a fair amount, but really only riding 5-10 miles a day for a few years, taking breaks during the winter, and always thinking it would be the summer of 2018—putting it off as long as I could before my 50th birthday—that I would quit my job (or take a 3+ month sabbatical) since my plan at the time was to ride from Washington to Maine, and the weather across the northern states is really only temperate enough for cycling during the summer.

I talked about it with everyone—friends, the kids, coworkers, strangers on a train—- but no one more than my husband, Randy. I would mention it at dinner, at the store, whenever I was going for a ride, whenever I had spent any portion of the day working on the plan. I talked about what I would eat and where we would stay, how I would stay safe and who would drive my SAG car. I talked about it for literally years, asking for opinions from where I should start and finish to whether I should bring dried foods and camp along the way.

I finally narrowed down the start and finish destinations to Westport, Washington and Kittery Point, Maine—a total of 3,700 miles, but despite many rants about "Someday" and how much I believe "doing it today" is the only way, the details were never more than hundreds of fantastical spreadsheets with how many miles I intended to ride each day from then until completion. Someday was still when I was going to do the ride, which of course you know means never.

In December of 2015 I was offered a job back in southern California the same week Randy was offered a job in American Fork, Utah. They were both too good to pass up, so we chose to take them and we would be together on the weekends by either flying or driving back and forth. In March 2016 Randy was going to Florida for a trade show. Instead of him flying out to see me in CA, he had me fly to Florida and we drove from Tampa down through the Keys. Florida in March is spectacular. It's humid, sure, but it's not hot yet, and the ocean breeze with your hand pretending to be an airplane out the window as you go across 107 miles of bridges and islands is practically the definition of perfection. You can look it up. If it doesn't say that, get a better dictionary.

I saw several people riding bikes across those bridges and the thought struck me that it would be cool if I rode to Key West instead of Maine—which would also expand the riding window from roughly three months of summer to at least seven since the southern states don't get snow, but it if added too many miles, I would just keep Maine as the destination.

From Westport, WA to Key West, FL is 3,800 miles using Google's bicycle directions. One hundred miles more, *and* I got to expand the riding window? Simplest decision ever, but even more than that, it threw gasoline on the fire and got me talking about it almost constantly. In late October of that same year, I left my job in SoCal and moved back to Utah with ideas of processing mortgages for 18 months or so and socking away cash, then quitting and executing my epic plan. In a moment of frustration, Randy said, "Are you ever really going to do this, or are you just having fun talking about it? Because if you're not, can we *please stop talking about it???"*

He was not trying to be rude. He was not meaning that it was a bad plan. I am so grateful he took the chance that I would be hurt by his blunt request because it kicked me in the cycling shorts and made *me* ask the other tough questions—including, "If this costs a *lot* of money, is that still going to be okay with you?"

The discussions were long, and not always fun, frankly. The reality was it was likely to cost $10,000 or more, and we didn't have any money currently saved to do it. Both the kids had moved out, so I didn't have a convenient support car driver if we wanted Randy to stay home and pay the rent, and we both liked our jobs, so quitting them and having to look for something else wasn't something we particularly wanted to do. After a particularly lengthy discussion, we effectively threw out all the "conventional rules", since I wasn't going for speed or a world record or anything—the ride was just about me wanting to do something *way* outside my comfort zone.

It was decided that we could take seven weeks off during the next two years and I could ride roughly 545 miles each "leg"; seven days of riding, Saturday to Saturday, with Sunday off.

We bought an even schmancier carbon-fiber bike for my birthday (since I wouldn't be carrying or trailering my gear behind me, a lighter bike was preferable), took the time off after Memorial Day, and on May 27, 2017 the adventure of a lifetime would begin.

When we're at a loss, we reach for the lowest bar— and the lowest bar is typically our highest level of training.

-Rachel Hollis, *Girl, Wash Your Face*

IF YOU CAN RIDE ACROSS TOWN, you can ride across the country.

-Peter Rice, *Spandex Optional Bicycle Touring*

One day, you will surely come across the Touring Trifecta:

Uphill, headwind, in the rain.

-Also Peter Rice. I put three quotes for this one. It's my book. I do what I want.

Chapter 10
Training

Here's the thing—call it a bike ride, I'll ride every possible day for as long as I can stand it. Call it "training" and I tire of it quickly most of the time. This time it was different. Almost as soon as we had the dates set up and the time off requested, I was in the gym 5 days a week for at least an hour. In retrospect, I should have ramped up a bit, but training for my first century ride hadn't bitten me *too* hard, so I should be fine, right?

Not so much. The key to training appropriately for an endurance athlete is work into the endurance piece *slowly*. Even if you're not overweight, which I have been for most of my adult life, and even if you've been doing endurance events previously, unless you are *currently, CONSISTENTLY* training, go slow.

I rode and rode on the stationary bike in the cold months and rode my bike to work 20+ miles as soon as I felt comfortable enough to do it (and willing to leave at 4:30-5:00 AM). Afternoons were too warm, plus I wasn't sure whether I could get back before dark after working all day, so I had to make sure I could leave my car the night before at the office. It took some strategic manipulation. I did do it several times, but I was lethargic every day. I have a severe reaction to caffeine that causes my stomach to produce way too much acid, so I couldn't do that anymore to combat the "sleepies", either.

Excerpt from the Blog (jypsyjillrides.com)

April 17, 2017—Good Friday

I'm sitting in my car sobbing like there's no tomorrow.

Today I worked really hard at work and was tempted to just go home and rest up for my 50 mile ride tomorrow. But my inner voice said, nah, you don't get to take a break during the cross country ride. Just do 10-15 miles.

Then traffic had me take a different route to the trail I ride on in the evening, and I was farther north than I usually start. I have a brand new bike, (thank you, Randy Peterson!) and

I got on the trail and headed north, thinking I'd turn around in 5 miles.

But I lost GPS and it didn't tell me how far I had gone until I got to 8, and I was feeling great, so decided 20 is a better number. But then the trail ended and I found myself on a super busy road in downtown Salt Lake. I considered for a moment continuing for the remaining mile to get to 10 before I turned around, but thought better of it and turned around.

1000 yards or so from where I turned around I was coming to a stop to cross the street and saw an obviously homeless man pulling a heavily loaded shopping cart with the saddest excuse for a bicycle I've seen in years. He was going pretty slow, but seemingly without reason his shopping cart overturned, taking him and his bike down in the middle of the road and spilling tent stakes, miscellaneous tools, and food from a cooler that popped open, all over the road.

A previously dark gray sky had just a few hints of blue popping through as he got up and yelled at the top of his lungs, "GOD, WHY ME?"

As I got within about 5 feet of the street, I hopped off my bike and asked if I could help him. He whirled around like I'd shot him. "WHERE DID YOU COME FROM? You weren't THERE a second ago."

I agreed and said, I was just out of sight when the cart turned over as we picked up the loose items and set them on the sidewalk. Then we lifted the cart together and got cart and bike to safety. He thanked me profusely and started to cry. "I'd almost just lost my faith. I've lost everything else. But then God sent an angel to tell me not to."

I told him I wasn't an angel, just a fellow traveler who was in the right place at the right time, and asked him if I could give him a hug. He agreed to that, and we hugged for a moment. I told him God would never stop believing in HIM, and that he was loved beyond imagination, even when he can't see it. I was wishing I had some money to give him. He thanked me again and I got on my bike. As I waited for the light to cross the street, I looked back and he was kneeling on the pile of everything he owned, and he said almost as loud as he had previously, "God? I'm sorry I asked why. Thank you for sending an angel."

As I rounded the corner to the park where I left my car I remembered that I'd put a $5 bill in my cycling pouch and was terribly upset that I hadn't remembered 9 miles ago.

I just opened the pouch, and there are two twenties, a ten, and a five where this morning I had put a five.

God must have wanted him to hear what I had to SAY more than what I had to GIVE.

GOOD Friday, indeed.

April 21, 2017 I turned 48 and training continued, but I was panicking. I knew I had in mind to ride 545 miles in seven riding days, and I was only averaging 18-20 miles per day with a longer day on Saturdays. I had never done anything its equal. I hid it as well as I could, though; laughing off discouragement and gradually increasing my endurance. I was working a full-time job, so I wasn't in a position to be able to train much more, and whatever happened would be what had to happen.

Ready or not, on May 26 we were in the car driving to Washington, with 545 miles planned.

The most miles I had ever ridden in a week was 254.

A bicycle ride around the world begins with a single pedal stroke.

– Dr. Scott Stoll—Avid Cyclist,   writer of the book *Falling Uphill*

CHAPTER 9
WESTPORT, WA TO KNEE INJURY AT GOVERNMENT CAMP, OR

STAGE STATS
START: 3,800 MILES TO KEY WEST
THIS STAGE STATS: 229 MILES, 4 DAYS, AVG MPH ~ 11.4

Morning came early May 27ᵗ, 2017. We had a 2 ½ hour drive from my brother-in-law Jon's house to Westport, and considering the impending heat, I needed to be riding by about 5AM. We took pictures of me with my rear tire in the surf, and I hoisted my bike up the sand dune and was on my way.

The first three-plus hours were glorious. I was within five miles of the coast for almost 40 miles, and in May, there is a dense mist that doesn't burn off until after 8AM or so. It makes breathing and staying cool easy. The only slight elevation changes as I stuck close to the coast made for a fairly simple ride, too.

At about the 54th (or so) mile, I was making my way up a pretty good incline and heard the familiar roar of a diesel pickup truck a little bit behind me. I always try to move over anytime a car is coming, but there was very little shoulder, so I couldn't get much farther to the right than I already was. As I heard the truck getting closer, my anxiety kicked in and I got even slower than I had been going, anticipating being "coal-rolled".

"Coal-rolling" is producing a highly unpleasant plume of black smoke. Some diesel pickup truck drivers have modified their exhaust in order to produce this at will, with which they have a tendency to take their frustrations (or flout their insecure masculinity, maybe? I've only ever seen it happen with guys at the wheel) out on drivers of hybrids, joggers, and cyclists.

Aside: Seriously guys, stop it. It's against the law, carries a hefty fine (between $200 and $5,000), and can cause fatal accidents when people cannot see through the exhaust.

I wished that this was all he had in mind. The driver slowed to roughly 10 mph and came very close to me (ignoring the 3-feet rule[9]), and tossed a beer bottle over the cab of the pickup as he sped up.—Fortunately, he produced only a little black smoke, and he wasn't very precise in his gauging how

[9] Nearly every state has laws that require motorists give cyclists ~ 3 feet of leeway on either side, regardless of where the cyclist is riding.

large his truck was. If his arc had been much higher, the bottle would have hit me square in the face. As it was, it hit the edge of the truck and shattered a foot or so in front of me. I would have swerved, but it happened so fast I couldn't even process what had happened. In that instant my fantastic illusions that this would be a perfectly safe and fun adventure were dashed. Because this happened so early in the ride, it had outsized importance to me. One jerk's actions meant to me that everyone on the road was either trying to kill me or at the very least finding me highly annoying, and I was tempted to throw in the towel at that point.

I tried to send Randy a text, but my cell service was sketchy in the area, and it wouldn't go through. So I was alone. I don't know if Randy would have actually hurt the guy if the text *had* gone through, (he was about 5 miles up the road, and easily could have flagged the guy down—there weren't many cars on that road that day) but I suspect it was good for everyone that it didn't. Knowing that I was alone didn't help me feel any better, though, and I sat on the side of the road and sobbed through my panic, doubting every plan, hope, and dream I'd had for the ride, and very much doubting myself.

Sitting on the side of the road for a few minutes, though, also reminded me that Randy was in reality a few miles away. It would be several more minutes—and probably at least half an hour—before he realized that I was going slower than usual and came to check on me. So I hiked to the top of the hill, got on the bike, and rode a few miles more without incident until I met up with Randy.

Shortly after that drama I was climbing another hill. Randy had warned me about, calling it "a heartbreaker." Because it was a local road and not a highway, the grade was not posted, but I'd told him about my experience with the bottle and how slow I'd been going, so he knew I'd need some encouragement and at least moral support. Fortunately, there were good patches of shade mixed in with the sun, but the hill's grade was significant enough that I really struggled. Eventually I was going so slowly that I had to get off the bike and walk up the hill. It was the first hill I'd had to walk on the ride, but it certainly wasn't the last. Walking when your intention is to ride all the way is demoralizing, and I was tired. I looked up the heartbreaking hill and thought, "Well, at least I don't have an audience while I'm walking."

It wasn't until I was about 10 feet from Randy, who was parked in the shade such that I couldn't see him (not on purpose, he just parked as far off the road as he could) that I realized he had been taking my picture all the way up to that point, and I still had 50-75 feet more before I would get to the top and could get back on the bike.

I was furious. What made him think I wanted to have photos of my ignominious defeat? I glared at him behind my sunglasses and kept going, and he kept taking pictures. When he sent them to my phone that evening I felt that shame all over again. The critic in my head said, "All hail the conquering hero—NOT." When I got to the one where I was bent over my bike, resting for a few seconds, I wished that I hadn't been so stupid as to make this silly goal to begin with. The next, where I was mounting the bike and heading down the other side, the critic was eerily silent as I recalled a favorite quote by Vincent Van Gogh: "If you hear a voice within you say, 'You cannot paint,' then by all means paint, and that voice will be silenced."

I went back to the pictures in the order they were taken, and looked at them slowly. One by one, they told me the story of a woman who dreamt of doing some great-but-likely-impossible thing, and it got hard. So she worked for it, and it got harder. She worked harder. She had to do it differently than she'd imagined, but she kept going. A champion stood at the top of the hill, but she knew that conquering the hill was not the end of the journey. So she caught her breath, left that particular challenge behind her, and pushed on.

I was not any more a champion that day than the day I imagined that crossing the country might be something I could do. Those pictures wouldn't show the same triumph as the photos in Key West. But like any great accomplishment, the first major hurdle I attempted, failed, and got back up to get past, defined and galvanized my ride, for that is where I learned that I would never—*NEVER*—stop moving forward until I was finished.

At the end of day one I wrote on the blog, "Happy Someday, everyone. Life is good. I'm happy tomorrow is a rest day."

Day Two I crossed into Oregon, which I will discuss in my segment on bridges, and rode through Portland. Fairly uneventful, but I was tender after my second day riding nearly 90 miles in up to 85-degree heat. Day three I was hurting and more tired than any time in recent memory, for sure, and possibly since recovering after a major surgery eight years prior.

Climbing into Government Camp (the base of Mount Hood) was miserable, although the cooling temperatures were a welcome change. There was a lot of construction in the area, and very misty conditions for miles and miles, but the mist gave me a good enough excuse to ride a little slower and only do 40 or so miles (as planned, since Google cycling directions indicated it would be a hefty climb of almost 4,000 feet).

Day four began at Government Camp. Despite the fact that it was the end of May, Mount Hood still had skiers on it, and we learned that Timberline Lodge runs the longest ski and snowboard season in North America—- often not closing at all. I got headed down the hill, and was enjoying the cool temperatures (it was 34°F outside at 8AM) when the road turned to an uphill slope. My right knee had been feeling irritated since day three, and I didn't look forward to climbing, but stood up in the saddle to charge up the hill I couldn't see the top of...

...and lost all power in my right leg. It didn't hurt at first, but it was obvious that something had gone terribly wrong. I continued to try, but as soon as my knee was bent more than about 15°, that knee would "pop", it hurt like someone had shoved a red-hot crowbar through my knee, and my muscles would not push or pull. Which meant that my left leg was having to work at double strength to keep me moving and upright. I got slower and slower, and in about 50 yards had so little momentum that I couldn't maintain uprightness, so I unclipped and started walking. I texted Randy and asked how far to the top, as there was something wrong with my leg, and let him know that I was walking. He came down to me, and I was limping severely. We made a snap decision to head to the next town instead of heading back toward Government Camp, as we weren't sure if there was a clinic or anything. In retrospect, skiing accidents happen all the time. Of *course* there's a place to seek medical attention. Hindsight…

Madras, Oregon has a clinic, but for injuries needing x-rays I needed to go to the emergency room. They had a full staff on hand, and on a Wednesday morning, very few emergencies, so I had the entire emergency department to myself for several hours. What they did not have was an orthopod or a CT machine. It was evident that I needed one, the other, or both, as the x-rays were inconclusive as to what I had injured in the soft tissue. At least nothing was broken. They put me in a brace and on crutches and I set up an appointment with an orthopedist at home on Friday. So we got in the car and headed to our next Airbnb and got some sleep before heading home in the morning.

BRIDGES

A few words about bridges. I knew when I signed up for this I would cross a bunch of them. I even knew about the bridges between all the islands in The Keys. That does not mean that I liked or looked forward to them. Probably my biggest fear is heights. I get dizzy standing on the third rung of a ladder longer than about 2 minutes, and in multiple attempts at

climbing higher than the third rung, have needed physical
assistance to come back down. I've been known to drive miles
out of my way to avoid overpasses.

The Lewis and Clark Bridge over the Columbia River
that goes from Longview, WA to Rainier, OR was unexpected. I
don't know what I thought was going to happen, but the first
major bridge I expected was over the Mississippi. But on Day
Two Randy had stopped in Longview and had food waiting and
a speech prepared for what I couldn't yet see.

"There's a pretty big bridge. I think I'd like to try and
get a good drone shot of you on it. You'll do great. Just keep
your mind on what you're doing and try to forget you're on a
bridge," he said.

I ate my sandwich and thought about how big this bridge
might be, and my strategies for bridges and overpasses in the
past: hold my breath, look only at the road 10-15 feet in front of
me, watch the white line. When I was finished with my snack I
got on the bike and Randy got the drone out and we parted,
again, with the encouragement of, "You'll do great."

The bridge revealed its 340 feet above the river and
1.569 miles long as I turned a corner past some trees and I
recognized that at least one of my strategies wasn't going to
work. Holding my breath for 8-10 minutes wouldn't do. So I
dropped back to the other two. Climbing the portion of the
bridge before I got to the water I could tell myself there was
land beneath me, so that worked for a little bit, but once I got
over the water, that confidence went away. I was still climbing,
so it felt like I was riding in slow motion, and then the reality of
the bridge hit. The Lewis and Clark Bridge is made of

corrugated metal, vertically fused together so it is somewhat like driving on millions of tiny straws. This is to keep the bridge from icing over in winter when the mists from the Columbia freeze. Looking at the white line or just in front of me I could see the water—or maybe it's a reflection of the water coming through the steel, but either way, the makeup of the bridge shot my final two bridge strategies down hard.

So I kept my body at an angle that had my eyes watching the license plates of the cars passing me. Not gonna lie, it sucked. I had no idea when I got to the flat portion of the bridge, nor when it started to slope downward. I only knew when I got to "real" road again, and I knew I'd made it.

Subsequent bridges were less challenging in many ways. The first major bridge was a surprise. The bridge over the Mississippi was almost as long, but not quite as high, and I'd ridden over half the country by then. My skin was a little thicker.

And then we got to the Keys: a series of islands off the southern tip of Florida conjoined by Highway 1. There are 42 bridges between Miami and Key West, spanning 113 miles. One of them is seven miles long. You've seen it in movies and on TV—License to Kill, True Lies, 2 Fast 2 Furious, and Burn Notice.

My last three days of riding crossed all 42 bridges. By the time I crossed The Seven Mile bridge on April 19, 2019, I was still slow, but confidently riding—looking at the water, looking at the birds, and watching the miles go by. There is a span near the center where the bridge rises to 65 feet for taller boat passage, and while I was climbing, I was passed by two other cyclists. The wind was coming from every direction, and I didn't hear them or notice until they were past me. I had long-since stopped feeling inadequate when others pass me on bicycles. It is what it is. But here's the thing: when I got to the end of the bridge, some 15-20 minutes later, those kind gentlemen were standing at the end, clapping and cheering like they knew who I was and what a challenge it was for me. This is the cycling community. What's not to love about that?

The lesson of bridges? Bridges are often the only way to get where you want to go. Certainly, despite the challenges, often the simplest. You, too, can turn your bridges into part of the joy of the journey.

You either love spinning the pedals and watching scenery whiz by, or you don't. And if you love it, not much can sour you on the idea of riding your bike.

-Sir Keith Mills, founder of Sported, and creator of Sky Miles.

CHAPTER 8
COMPOUNDING INJURIES

Even without an MRI the orthopedist was able to diagnose a severely torn MCL (the inside ligament of the knee). He ordered physical therapy, and to stay on the crutches until the therapist said I was ready to get off them. He also stated that professional football players are typically back on the field no sooner than six weeks from this type of injury. "So be good, and we will reassess in six weeks."

I had been mentally prepared for him to say, "Yeah… maybe you should take up knitting instead of all this craziness. Don't you know how old you are?" so that was some relief.

That was June 2. On Saturday, June 10 I was working some overtime and got a call from my friend James McFee. We knew each other through work when I was in California. After a fair amount of hemming and hawing, he divulged that he had taken quite a few pills and didn't want to wake up. I tried everything I could to get him to tell me where he was or to call

911, or something. To no avail. When we hung up several hours later he was losing consciousness and I couldn't stop crying until I got home. I had tried to think of anyone to call, but not knowing where he was other than probably the state of California, I didn't know what to do. So I prayed and begged God to have someone find him before it was too late.

I didn't know his family or friends, though I'd met his fiancée, but I only knew her first name. I didn't have contact information for anyone who would know how to reach his people. On Tuesday, June 13, I arrived to an email from another of his coworkers to call or text her on her cell phone. Before I made the call I knew what she was going to say. My hope that his "radio silence" the past two days had been because someone found him and got him help in time was in vain. James was gone.

All humans try to make sense of death. At funerals and in obituaries and when we speak of the dead, we say, "It was their time." "God had a bigger plan." "They're in a better place." Perhaps all of that is true, but I think more than anything it helps it make sense to us.

Death by suicide is a different kind of grieving. It isn't possible to make sense of someone dying who was 34, or 15, or 22. It isn't possible to make sense of someone dying who wasn't sick, who had goals and dreams for their life, is in love, and seemingly has so much to live for. Even the rote explanations don't make sense of anything. (They don't actually make sense of anything when you're on the grieving end of *any* death, but that's an entirely other book.) When a friend or family member dies by suicide it introduces a special kind of hell. The person is no less dead, but every day is littered with "what-ifs" and "why?" and an anger and sadness that never goes away.

On June 24, I went to the memorial for James in California. I couldn't speak, even during the portion of the memorial where it was opened to everyone who wanted to do so. There were too many words, too much anger; it was just too raw to expose to the light of day. What I would have said if I could have processed it at the time is this: I'm sad that my friend died. I'm sad that he thought this was the only way to fix the myriad of problems he had created and the thousands of chips that had fallen because of the decisions he had made. I'm angry that it took him calling me to open my eyes to the fact that I was dealing with the anger, depression, and anxiety I had felt for years in silence, only confiding in a few select people I believed would not take advantage of my vulnerability, and my silence would likely end up leading me down the same path.

I am so, *SO* grateful that his final call was, for me, a true wake-up call. Now I know that I don't get to protect those I love from the upsetting news that I am depressed, or anxious, or sad, or feeling super low on my lowest days, simply because it may make them uncomfortable. Uncomfortable is *nothing* in comparison to the pain that will follow everyone who knew him for the rest of their lives. The two days of fearful radio silence when I had a shred of hope were bliss compared to the feeling that I could have or should have done something more.

Choosing whether I speak up when I am feeling low is literally a matter of life or death. I get to choose life. I get to choose to ask for help, over and over, and over again if I need it.

Scream it if I must until I know that I have been heard, and when it bubbles up again, make sure I know I'm heard again. Even if it doesn't help and it continuously bubbles, knowing that I am not alone in the storm helps me to keep strong in the hope that it will get better and easier. I only need to look at my new friends—family of James—to be reminded that regardless of the anger and frustration and true *harm* he caused them, they will never be the same without him here. They all want to go back in time and return it to what it was before. I cannot *ever* allow my mind to get all the way to the point that my mind cries out that people would be better off without me.

> Please, dear reader: if you are ever in the middle of your own personal hell, reach out. Talk. Ask. Beg. I am begging you to stay. During one of your "breaks" when you are feeling a little more solid, promise someone you love that if you get to the point where you are considering this final decision, you will call them. Make that connection with another person. Make them promise the same to you. To this point, you have fought successfully through 100% of your worst days. Promise your loved one you'll tell them when your worst day does hit. And know that you are loved. By so many of us. I may not even know you, and I love you. Your life means something. Make it mean something amazing. On your worst day, ask your person what your life means to them, and truly listen. They'll tell you what they want to say at your funeral. Just. *Stay*.

Physical therapy was tough that first week before James died, but while it was painful, the therapist seemed to be going for "ease her in" rather than "fix it." The week *after* he died, when I was "broken in," was a different story. She would say, "tell me if it gets too much" and my response was always, "I'm never going to tell you it's too much. The worse it is, the sooner I'm back on the bike." My eyes filled with tears as the pain in my friend's last words filled my mind, drowning out the pain in my knee.

On July 11 after several PT appointments, 7 weeks of rest and more stretching and strengthening of the legs, I was cleared to ride, with the stipulation that I needed to start "small" (not more than 40 miles at a time, and only one day at a time) and work my way up to longer distances in subsequent weeks. The therapist had also explained what I should do when the knee acts up, and why it might act up even if the knee was fine, but something else was needing attention; the body knows the pain in the knee was what stopped me the last time. So for the next year or more, if I had pain in my knee, it could mean anything from dehydration to hunger, to stretching, to something not sitting right in my stomach, to a rock in my shoe; it could be literally almost anything. So if I had a twinge of pain in my knee, I needed to attack it with everything: get a drink, eat, stretch, take my shoes off and stretch my feet, etc. All strategies changed, and my focus of each ride was to have a plan before I started, stop more often, and truly pay attention to what my body was asking for.

> *It doesn't matter if you're sprinting for an Olympic gold medal, a town sign, a trailhead, or the rest stop with the homemade brownies. If you never confront pain, you're missing the essence of the sport.*

-Scott Martin—Team USA, 2016 Paralympian Cyclist and Marine Corps Veteran

CHAPTER 7
BACK IN THE SADDLE

STAGE STATS
229 MILES IN, 3,571 TO GO
1,099 MILES, 19 DAYS,
AVG MPH ~ 11.8

Folks, believe me when I say that "starting small" when you've got 80+ mile days in your rear-view feels like failure. You don't get the "I've really done something" feeling that you're craving. It's just a long Saturday ride. I consistently taped my knee and took breaks about every 12-15 miles to stretch, eat, and rest.

Because I wouldn't be able to immediately attack a week at a shot until I was healed, we broke up nearly 500 miles into 8 weekend trips over the next three months. On the Saturdays I wasn't on the route I trained on the roads and trails near my home. Each day I rode, the pain would take longer to materialize, until eventually I could go for 20 miles or more, depending on hills. Climbing was occasionally still a challenge, and it took me almost a year from the initial injury to remember that standing up from the saddle during a climb was a good idea; a great deal of power is in body weight, and the muscles are diminished in their power if I am sitting on them. I was also terrified to stand up, because I associated the injury with the climbing, and not the 230 miles I had ridden before I was fully prepared.

One of the unpleasant things about Utah and Idaho is the unchanging scrub and badland. I have driven and ridden those roads what feels like hundreds of times, if not thousands, over the years. I've driven them even more since I began using Friday drives to give me an early biking start on Saturday. Driving these long, straight roads feels interminable at 80 mph (don't freak out, it's the speed limit out there!), and that is even though in a car there is air conditioning, plus if I get bored and I'm not driving I can sleep. This is good, because the landscape looks very much the same, for more than 500 miles.

From the Blog:
July 23, 2017

Friday traffic is ridiculous on Pioneer Day (a Utah holiday, celebrating the entry of the original pioneers who came here in wagon trains and handcarts) weekend. We got as far as the Wal-Mart distribution center in Corinne (Utah) Friday before I got on the bike to head to our hotel. I might have gone farther if it wasn't going to be so late when I got to the hotel, but I suspect that would have been unwise since it was about 10 billion degrees outside. (okay, not really, but much earlier and it was 99) So 9.5 miles on Friday night.

Then yesterday I got up early and rode before daybreak. I was 20 miles into the (planned) 54 before dawn started to peek out over the mountains and enjoying the relative cool. At 49 miles in, the Legacy Parkway trail just suddenly stopped, and the GPS had a hard time rerouting me. That cut my pace substantially, because I had no idea other than, "south" where I was going.

Ultimately it only added 1/2 a mile to the ride, and though there were some harrowing moments when I found myself in between the merge of a freeway off-ramp and the road I chose, (sorry, mom...) I was done with my 54.5 miles before 9:30 AM and home before 10.

Discovered Facebook Live in the last couple of weeks—see the videos on my feed there. I love that I can show some of the scenery I'm riding through—looking up. I don't adjust the position of the camera much because I don't want to lose my phone from the holster I keep it in on my bike, but if you want to see some of the things I see, take a gander over there.

:) 347 miles in. 9 percent of the way done. Next week I will be done with 10.5 percent. :)

In order to facilitate my recovery, we tweaked the plan slightly and decided the segments of the ride could be done out of order. Roughly every other Saturday, Randy and I would head out to the last place we left off and whittle off the miles between Boise, Idaho and our home in Lehi, Utah. We did this for two months. By Labor Day weekend (the first Monday in September) I had burned away all the miles between Nampa, Idaho and Lehi, Utah, and we went back to conquer the remaining 391 miles of Oregon.

Randy got a little weary sometimes of being gone every other weekend or so, and he occasionally had things he had to do (like work conferences), so I would take d'Artagnan most of those times. Two of the weekends, though, my father-in-law Chuck came (first with Randy, then on his own) and followed me for the miles between Nampa, Idaho and Mountain Home, Idaho. I had some fun conversations with Chuck when I was in the car with him or on breaks—- on a particularly desolate stretch (it's all pretty bleak in the summer out there), I saw miles and miles of wild sunflowers, but only on one side of the road, and almost like they were planted there in rows. I asked why he thought that might be?

He pointed at the power lines above that side of the road. When he saw my confused look, he said, "Sunflower seeds are super popular in bird seed. The birds sit on the power lines and poop. And bird poop is good fertilizer for the not-quite-digested sunflower seeds." I could almost hear and see a star with a trailing rainbow shoot across the screen in my mind with someone singing, "The More You Know…" Any time I saw wild sunflowers on the side of remote roads I looked for the power lines, and he was right, every time.

From the blog:
8/5/2017

Okay, the "easy" plan using Google Maps turned out to be... not so great. Love Google's interface, just not so much the execution. If it has a name, Google will tell you that you can ride it on a bicycle. Even if the pavement turns into a dirt road... that goes through an Air Force bombing range... (just outside Mountain Home Air Force Base, Bruneau, Idaho)

Lest you think I rode *through* the bombing range, I didn't. The sign literally says objects may fall from aircraft. We re-mapped and put me on the frontage road between Mountain Home and Glenn's Ferry.

I crashed near Eden, Idaho when I shifted too quickly to climb a hill. My chain locked, and I couldn't get unclipped quickly enough to avoid it. I could tell I wasn't *badly* injured, but it had knocked the wind out of me, and the remnants of the wild grasses that had recently been cut had scratched my arms and legs. After lying there for 2-3 minutes catching my breath, I discovered that I am slightly allergic to whatever grasses (or pesticides they put on it) were there, because I broke out in tiny hives.

In Burley, Idaho I struggled with intense heat. All of you, "but it's a dry heat!" people? Ugh. And I do mean *UGH*. 102 degrees is hot, whether it's in an oven or a hot tub (max recommended temperature according to Google is 104 for those bad boys!), and it was 102 in the shade that day, with no wind and not a cloud in the sky. Oh, and farmland (potatoes, alfalfa, and cattle grazing, mostly) on every side, so no shade for 98% of the 60 miles for that day.

Trying to stay hydrated when you're riding for almost 6 hours and the temperature hits 90 before 8AM is near impossible; you're not only racing the sun, you're racing your own biology, because dehydration can quickly lead to heat exhaustion and heat stroke, which is a full-blown medical emergency that can cause permanent organ damage and death.

After we again remapped the planned route on the fly in order to avoid dirt roads, Randy and I got onto two different routes. He hadn't realized we were heading to different places, and when I finished it took him a few minutes to get to me. So I laid down in someone's grass under one of their trees and fell quickly asleep. The owner of the home came out to see if I was okay, and I pretended I was fine, but my heart was racing and my tongue and toes were tingling. Randy got there and helped me stand up and walk to the car, but my muscles were weak and my joints felt like they were held together with peanut butter. As soon as I got cooled down and was able to catch my breath, the symptoms went away, but it was scary knowing that I had heat exhaustion and could have done myself some significant damage.

The Idaho/Utah State Line was a great day—one of my fastest 55 mile rides ever, at 3:45. The first 25 miles was downhill, and a decent slope at that. The remaining 30 I completed almost on sheer momentum. It was mostly flat, and I'd been able to ride without expending much energy, so it was great to start that week with 55 miles at almost 15 mph. That was the Friday before Labor Day, 2017. On Saturday I rode

Vale to Nampa, Idaho, and Sunday we drove to Government Camp to complete the last miles of Oregon and Idaho.

For the aforementioned trip between Vale, Oregon and Nampa, Idaho (70 miles), we were close enough to Boise that mom came and drove a portion so that Randy could ride half of them with me. That was a lot of fun. Mom was afraid she would do it "wrong," but she did fantastically. I learned from that situation that often when you are feeling doubtful, it is okay to jump in and do your best. Most of the time you will be just fine, and "done" is better than perfect. Often there isn't even a perfect way to *do* what you're wanting to do. So rather than strive for the unattainable, just get it done. That was also the last day Randy had anything to say about whether I was fast or slow, or gave me tips on riding technique, because he got a greater appreciation for how long and how far I was going day after day.

The first week of September in Oregon is always going to be warm. 2017 was especially warm, and with 1,069 wildfires burning during that month in that state *alone*, it was dubbed "Smoketember." We woke up at 2AM and rode before it started to get hot and the smoke became oppressive. I've never been a smoker, but the effects of *any* smoke on my body were evident, both with breathing and my heart rate. I soaked a head sock with water and put it around my mouth so there was a little bit more of a filter, but the benefits were minimal after 10-15 minutes, because it would dry out so quickly.

Because it was the middle of the night, Randy would follow close behind me—within 25-30 feet—with his flashers on so that if someone was driving on the road at that early hour, they would see him for sure and have to go around me, whereas they might not even notice me with flashing bicycle lights in the dark if I were alone. There were times the smoke was so thick that my shadow looked like two gigantic cyclists (one shadow from each headlight) projected on a screen in front of me. Though I knew it was a trick of the lighting, it was comforting to feel like I wasn't alone in my struggles to climb and to complete the day's ride before it got too hot.

Even with the smoke and heat, the eastward miles between Government Camp and Burns, Oregon were amazing. After Mount Hood the landscape looks much like southern Idaho and Utah—lots of sagebrush and dirt. On Friday, September 8, I knew I had some climbing ahead of me. We were farther away from the fires, so the smoke was less oppressive, but while Google maps gives you an indication that there *is* climbing, it isn't particularly accurate as to how *much* climbing there is. After a grueling three mile climb and five mile *descent*, I stopped to refuel (a la, peanut butter sandwiches!—thank you Sesame Street and The Amazing Mumford) and gear up for the remaining 25 or so miles. A police officer stopped and asked if we needed any help. We explained what was going on, and he said, "Ah, so you just did the Stinkingwater climb. That's a doozy. Are you doing the Drinkwater today, or waiting until tomorrow?"

I had no idea. I told him how much farther I was going, and he said I had the Drinkwater ahead of me. Apparently the Stinkingwater is 1,200 feet or so of climbing over three or so miles. The Drinkwater is "only" 1,100 feet or so of climbing, but is one and a quarter miles. He was not remotely exaggerating. I had used just about all I had to get over the Stinkingwater pass, and there was nothing in the tank for the Drinkwater.

From the base, the Drinkwater doesn't look like much; just a bit of a climb with a right turn, with the road beyond obscured by trees and shrubs. But it is deceptive, since you're on a bit of a slope before you get to the main upturn, and you don't really notice because it was so gradual leading up to it.

If my legs had been given a night's rest prior, I might have made it to the first turn. I got about 75 yards up and my knee started to complain. I pushed it as far as I could, since once I'm off the bike, I'm walking the rest of the way up, but 50 yards or so later, I was off, angry and tired.

I stretched and got the "hitch" in my knee worked out, and started walking. To my right there was a beautiful view of the valley below, but I was irritated enough with myself that I could barely appreciate how lovely it was. About 50 yards after I started walking there was a large bull elk standing just on the other side of the guardrail, grazing on some of the tall grass. If I'd had some of that grass in my hand I suspect he would have eaten it from me without blinking. He didn't care about me any more than the thousands of cows I'd already passed along the way had, barely looking up as I walked past. I did end up startling him, though, as I got farther up the road and every part of my body hurt—I started talking to myself and he sure didn't like that. I heard him head down the slope shortly after.

Talking to myself turned quickly into yelling at myself (drill sergeant style), then praying, then bargaining with God, then just crying, since none of it was helping. My knee wasn't complaining anymore, but everything else was, including the bone right behind my ears, where the helmet straps had been being pressed by the sunglasses for more than five hours that day. My walking had slowed to roughly 1 mile per hour, and I knew Randy was waiting at the top of the pass for me, but at the rate I was going, it would be a full hour before I got there. Another fifty or so yards of crying and thinking I should just quit, I looked up the hill to see if I'd made more progress than it felt like I had, and saw Randy running down the hill toward me.

If you've never felt like a character in a movie or TV show who believed that they were about to die, but the cavalry showed up to save the day, this might be a foreign concept to you, but I knew at that moment that I was going to be okay. It didn't change the height or length of the climb, but I wasn't going to be alone, and Randy would help me.

When he got to me he asked what he could do. I had him just push the bike, which I believed was part of the reason I was so slow. I didn't realize how right I was. My whole body was tired, so I was leaning on the bike, with my spine at a skewed angle. With every step, the muscles in my arms, legs, back, torso, and even feet tightened, causing miniature charley horse cramps all over my body. As soon as I could stand up straight and walk like a human being again, I wasn't in nearly the pain, and we walked up the rest of the hill together. I was also able to talk through the physical and emotional turmoil and Randy told me jokes and made teasing comments that were distractions from the discomfort during the trek up the hill.

I rested for a few minutes at the top, and Randy prepped the drone to take a long descent shot. The view was glorious, followed by a fast descent into Juntura. With only one day left of riding for that leg, I knew I would make it at least to Vale, even as sore as I was.

By the end of 2017, I had also completed some more of the Utah miles as well as a quick trip down New Mexico way over Thanksgiving, and was 1,336 miles into the journey, with a solid plan on how to have the full first half completed before Memorial Day, 2018.

From the blog:
Sept 3, 2017

So there are 11 states I'll be riding through on this journey of a lifetime: Washington, Oregon, Idaho, Utah, Colorado, New Mexico, Texas, Louisiana, Mississippi, Alabama, and Florida.

As of today I have ridden all of the miles in two of them. (Washington and Idaho)

If all goes as planned, Oregon will be complete by the end of the week.

Yesterday was my fastest 55 miles in many years at 3 hours 45 minutes. It was a good downhill for the first 25 miles, and I was feeling good. Then as I was getting to Malta, Idaho a large dog chased me for about a mile, barking within inches of my heels, and I had to push myself harder than usual to keep from being bitten. By the time he gave up I had expended so much energy it was tough to complete the remaining 18 or so miles, but I did, of course.

Today's was 68 miles. Mom came with us to see what this thing was all about and there was a HUGE fringe benefit that let Randy have some time on the road with me. She did a fantastic job, too. (Just like Chuck did last week!)

Anyway, Randy was a trooper. He got 35 miles rocked out, and hasn't been on a bike in almost a year. It was awesome having him along—literally—for the ride. That said, he's hurting this evening. He may have overdone it a little. I'm more exhausted than hurting.

Rest day tomorrow (and travel to Mount Hood). Happy riding, everyone, and have a LOVELY Labor Day.

Sept 10, 2017

On the bicycle route there are 1,024 miles between Westport, WA and Lehi, UT. On May 27, 2017 I started riding in Westport. The injury on May 31 put a 6 week hiatus on cycling while my knee recovered, so we regrouped and decided to do the route in snippets instead of one long "thread." On Saturdays since I was cleared to ride I did the miles between Nampa, ID and Lehi, UT. Then last Saturday (Sept. 2) got the miles done between Vale, OR and Nampa, leaving 329 miles, all in Oregon, to complete by today.

There were days this week that felt frustratingly long and slow, and the days that I thought, man, I could ride all day today—though I'm glad I stopped when I did.

Today's highlight was how it ended. I'd only been on the bike for about 3.5 hours and the only significant climb of the day was almost done. I knew I was close, because the GPS said I had two miles left. As I crested the hill and Randy was at the top, he stopped me and asked which shot I'd like him to get— (will upload probably sometime tomorrow) and we agreed to which one we thought would be the best one, he got the drone into place, and I headed toward the downhill as my music changed songs. Now, don't judge me for my music selection on this playlist. Almost any song with a good beat or inspiring message can make my list.

Whitney Houston's One Moment in Time from the 1988 Olympics started. And yes, I was flying down that hill. (the video may or may not bear that out, but suffice it to say I was.) Two miles of downhill goes pretty quick on a bike, and it's kind of a long song, so it was just finishing up as I hit the bottom and slowed down. It's been hitting me all day that I've done something pretty incredible—mom said it best, though it's a little surreal. So here are the statistics and charts:

1,024 miles

Approximately 90 hours on the bike

Approximately 29,314 feet of climbing

Approximately 24,774 feet of downhill (the fun part...
lol)

26.9% of 3,800 miles total complete

41% of the total climbing

Now I'm going to rest for a few weeks and do some more miles after some planning and some more training.

Thanks for all your encouragement and love from across the miles! I couldn't do it without you. :)

I don't ride a bike to add days to my life. I ride a bike to add life to my days.

-Unknown

CHAPTER 6
COLORADO BORDER TO OLTON, TX

STAGE STATS
1,298 MILES IN,
2,502 MILES TO GO
584 MILES, 10 DAYS,
AVG MPH 11.9
HALFWAY

From the blog:
Aug 19, 2017

Well the morning was BEAUTIFUL.

Hammett Hill, (near Mountain Home, Idaho) however, was still 25 miles ahead of me, and it's a 6% grade for a full mile. I'd killed several hills leading up to it, and was feeling good, but about 1/4 mile into the climb my legs were on fire and I was a little nervous about not being able to get unclipped and crashing again, so I got unclipped and started walking. Kept thinking I was almost to the top only to discover there was more hill. This is on the Oregon Trail Road. It crosses the Oregon Trail several times, and the damage to the earth after more than 150 years is still evident. But I have a healthy respect for those Pioneers, who braved the wild WITHOUT bicycles and paved roads and Mapquest and the support vehicle bringing them ice water, protein bars and encouragement. It is during the hardest parts that I recognize that there is NO WAY I'm doing this crazy thing without my intense support group.

So for that support, I thank each of you. I thank Randy all the time, of course. He's in the trenches with me. But also those following my progress. I think of you on these long rides. Your comments and encouragement are helping me along.

The last week of January, 2018 I got laid off with 35 of my friends. When Randy and I were discussing what I should do next we concluded that I would attend a QA Software Engineering class, and change the industry in which I was working. We live in one of the fastest growing tech corridors in the nation here in Utah, and I wanted in.

Since I had a few weeks before the course started, we headed out to Texas to get some miles in over President's Day week. I had barely hit Olton (roughly halfway between Westport and Key West) when a cold front rolled in, dropping the temperature to 18 degrees (-8C). We stayed another full day, hoping the cold would break and I would be able to get a few more days of riding in, but the forecast was for cold and worse through the weekend, so we packed it in and headed home with 448 miles to go in the first half.

The QA class was tough, but it was not nearly as frustrating as the next four months of job hunting. Seventeen interviews, at least half of which I felt went really well, came and went, often with the recruiter calling me back and saying, "They really liked you, but have chosen another candidate." I drove for Uber to keep from getting stir crazy, stayed focused on the goal, and tried to stay positive. Finally the call came, and because I was waiting in a parking lot and didn't want to turn off the Uber app, almost didn't answer the phone. A software company was offering me a QA job, and I would start August 6.

By the day I started working I had only ridden a total of 1,780 miles on route—120 miles short of halfway—and I had only 260 days to finish the ride if I was going to do so before my birthday. Because I didn't believe I could earn enough time off before my birthday, I stretched the goal out to the year of my 50th birthday, knowing that I wouldn't be able to earn enough time off in the last ⅓ of 2018 and the first ⅓ of 2019 to get me there. But the company (and God, really) had other things in store for me.

Company policy is that full time employees' paid time off (PTO) is "front-loaded", which is to say, the day I started I had 7 days of PTO I could use whenever I wanted through the end of the year. And on January 1 I would have seventeen days of PTO I could take at any time during the year. I couldn't believe it. In the first three weeks of work, I kept going back to HR to make sure I understood correctly. This meant that not only could I finish in 2019, I could finish before my birthday in 2019. Which was exciting, until it wasn't.

I still didn't actually believe it was going to happen, even having come 1,780 miles. It always felt like I'd end up "wussing out" or having an accident or injury, or that we'd realize that it was taking too much money, or whatever. All of a sudden when the excitement went away and it hit me that I had no more excuses to not be done before my birthday, it was daunting. I picked up the last of the Colorado and New Mexico miles over the 2018 Labor Day weekend, officially crossing off the last of the first half on September 3, 2018—with 230 days to go, I had roughly 1,878 miles left to ride, and 24 PTO days to get them done.

The Utah miles (all driveable from home, so I did them on weekends) were some of the toughest climbs and had some of the most amazing scenery. I'd seen it hundreds of times, but never so slowly, so I hadn't appreciated it fully. There's a lesson in this that I didn't get until a specific event later.

My route through Utah involved the infamous Highway 6. Highway 6 runs between Spanish Fork and Green River, and is roughly 120 miles of climb and descent through a canyon of Carbon County. (As in, coal mining country. As one of my Uber riders noticed, "I guess they don't call these mountains the Rocky Mountains for nothing!") According to Wikipedia, "the 120 miles (190 km) section of US 6 between Spanish Fork and Green River is considered one of the deadliest stretches of highway in the United States. A high volume of trucks and automobiles travel that stretch at interstate speeds, along hairpin turns, through narrow canyons." I have known this for many years, and was nervous, to say the least, about riding a bicycle on them.

The riding day (Day 23—Dec 2, 2017) between Tie Fork Rest Area and Wellington, UT (46 miles) was the day I dreaded. There was some good climbing, but the downhill was the piece I most feared, as that was the part with the hairpin turns and where the road becomes the narrowest as well. It isn't a very long distance, considering, but with the severity of the climbs, they were nothing to sneeze at either. The weather wasn't in my favor, although there wasn't any snow in the forecast and it hadn't snowed in several days, so that was a good thing.

I got up and down a few bits of the ride, and was heading up a good 450 foot or so climb. My whole body was hurting. I was really only about 15 or so miles in, so that didn't make much sense to me, but I'd hunkered down against the wind and cold, and between the cold and the fear of potential traffic my muscles were more tense than usual. Thankfully, it wasn't too bad because it wasn't a holiday, and the big trucks tend to detour around the canyon when it gets colder in case there is ice.

Because it was below 50 degrees the entire ride, my body was trying to conserve heat and energy as much as possible. I was angry and crying and praying for help to make it up the hill without having to walk, when I heard my dad's voice say, "Look up." I moved my eyes up the hill a little bit, and immediately felt more discouraged—how was I going to make it up that beast?—and heard his voice again say, "LOOK. UP." So I lifted my chin and looked at the rocks and the strata lines. I looked at the crystal-clear blue of the sky. I looked at the Price River and the railroad tracks. And as I did so, my position shifted slightly. My shoulders dropped. My back straightened. My knees were able to extend more fully. And I got to see more beauty.

Sometimes when we're stressed we get so tied up in our situation that we forget to look up. Whether that's looking up to God and asking for help or looking up from our desks to see all the good things that have happened, or looking up from the hole that we've dug for ourselves enough to know that there is beauty all around us. Don't forget to LOOK UP.

WEATHER

"Fair-weather riding is a luxury reserved for Sunday afternoons and wide boulevards. Those who ride in foul weather—be it cold, wet, or inordinately hot—are members of a special club of riders who, on the morning of a big ride, pull back the curtain to check the weather and, upon seeing rain falling from the skies, allow a wry smile to spread across their face. This is a rider who loves the work."—Velominati (a cycling webpage)

We had decided our best bet was to do stages, and the more time off we could plan around national holidays, the better. Wisdom dictated that we take into account the general weather patterns in the 12 states I would traverse, so those also came into play. New Mexico, Texas, Louisiana, Mississippi,

Alabama, Georgia and Florida could be done in traditionally cooler months, while Washington, Oregon, Idaho, Utah and Colorado would need to be done in the Spring, Summer, and early Fall. But it gets tricky, because there are also localized weather pattern "seasons" once you get past Albuquerque or so. Peak tornado season is March through June in the midwest states, and hurricane season is June through November in the south.

An example: September 1, 2018 I rode the 69 miles of the southwestern corner of Colorado. We left dark and early in the morning. I couldn't tell how much of a storm there was, but it was definitely overcast. Within five minutes of my start it was raining, though not hard.

I had planned for a chilly morning and was wearing my windbreaker reflective gear, but its chill-reducing properties are reduced to nothing when wet, and soon hail was pelting my arms and legs, with no dulling protection from a heavier cloth. Hail is typically not long-lasting, and fortunately it was pretty small, but then it turned into snowflakes for a minute or two.

My cycling shoes are made of carbon fiber, with very little padding, so as to keep the feet cool and the skin breathing, but that also means they get really cold really quickly in inclement weather. So I was soaked to the skin, with snow falling—though not sticking, thank goodness—and more than a little bit uncomfortable. By the time the snow turned into sleet I was shivering and miserable.

I gave myself one more mile, and then I would have to wait out the storm in the car. Before the mile was complete, the storm above me had stopped, and the sun had come out. The entire remaining 60+ miles I could see storm systems all around me, with flashes of lightning in the distance and the thunder rolling subtly a few seconds later, but I got no more rain.

When we stopped at the New Mexico border we drove south. The plan was to stay in Farmington overnight and ride the "gap" miles between the New Mexico border and where I had left off in NAPI HQ, NM, completing the 1,900 miles between Westport, WA and Olton TX, in the morning. As we crossed the border we were hit with a dust storm so massive we had to pull over on the side of the freeway and wait for enough visibility to see cars 10 feet in front of us on the road. I was very grateful I wasn't riding in it.

Texas was a mixed bag of stale air, wind, below-freezing cold, and blazing hot. No snow, but very windy. I wasn't prepared with warm enough gear for anywhere close to that cold, so we hung out for a day to see if it would change. When it didn't, and the forecast was equally daunting, we headed home. In November 2018 we were back in Texas and it was perfect until the last day, which I will detail later, but the bottom line is—I outran a tornado. How's that for a teaser?

Florida was scorching hot even in February. We would get up early and ride before dawn at least half the miles for the day. As I got closer to the larger, more-populated cities, Randy stayed pretty close, sort of leap-frogging every ten miles or so (better description in chapter five) since we didn't really know how bad the weather/traffic would be. Once we got to the Keys, the weather was amazing due to the ocean breezes, but the wind was crazy on the Seven Mile Bridge, and I couldn't tell which direction it was coming from. "Sleeping in" until 6:00 AM felt like an island gift, and my body certainly relished it.

Weather has a lot more factors than just atmospheric events like rain and wind, however. In Oregon there were fires, and the "dry heat" was worse than the humid heat east of the Mississippi. Any time it got hotter than 70 degrees I hit diminishing returns more quickly and it got harder to tell what my body was telling me. The "lesson" of the weather is this: do whatever you can to make your decisions early in the game. When you're in the heat of it, under stress, or otherwise focused, it is a lot more difficult to make a good decision.

Stops, Dates, and Miles

Riding Day	Day's Stop	Date	Day's Miles	Avg. mph
1	Vader, WA	5/27/2017	91	10.5
2	Gresham, OR	5/29/2017	90	13.0
3	Government Camp, OR	5/30/2017	41	10.1
4	Lehi, UT	7/15/2017	40	9.3
5	SLC, UT	7/22/2017	55	11.1
6	Brigham City, UT	7/29/2017	81	12.4
7	Burley, ID	8/12/2017	61	8.9
8	Wendell, ID	8/19/2017	71	9.6
9	Mountain Home, ID	8/26/2017	65	13.1
10	UT/ID State Line	9/1/2017	55	15.2
11	Nampa, ID	9/2/2017	53	11.1
12	Madras, OR	9/4/2017	64	10.5
13	Prineville, OR	9/5/2017	31	9.5
14	Hampton, OR	9/6/2017	68	10.2
15	Burns, OR	9/7/2017	68	11.9
16	Juntura, OR	9/8/2017	58	10.1
18	Orem, UT	9/16/2017	17	9.4
19	Tucker, UT	10/28/2017	45	11.4

20	Cline's Corners, NM	11/23/2017	61	10.1
21	Fort Sumner, NM	11/24/2017	102	16.2
22	Taiban, NM	11/25/2017	20	9.5
23	Wellington, UT	12/2/2017	43	11.3
24	Albuquerque, NM	2/17/2018	44	10.6
25	Muleshoe, TX	2/19/2018	71	13.4
26	Olton, TX	2/20/2018	36	9.8
27	Moab, UT	3/17/2018	49	10.6
28	San Ysidro, NM	3/31/2018	75	13.7
29	Counselor, NM	5/5/2018	63	12.1
30	CO/UT Border	5/19/2018	72	11.6
31	Green River, UT	6/2/2018	57	14.8
32	CO/NM Border	9/1/2018	69	10.7
33	Napi HQ, NM	9/3/2018	48	13.8
34	Lockney, TX	11/22/2018	41	12.2
35	Paducah, TX	11/23/2018	85	15.1
36	Seymour, TX	11/24/2018	80	9.8
37	Megargel, TX	11/25/2018	23	15
38	Springtown, TX	11/26/2018	84	11.4
39	Garland, TX	11/27/2018	71	9.7
40	Mineola, TX	11/28/2018	79	9.9

41	Marshall, TX	11/29/2018	68	10.4
42	Ringgold, LA	11/30/2018	73	10.3
43	Winnfield, LA	12/1/2018	55	10.6
44	Jonesville, LA	2/14/2019	60	11.9
45	Lucien, MS	2/15/2019	76	9.8
46	Hattiesburg, MS	2/16/2019	92	10.5
47	Wilmer, AL	2/18/2019	75	10.7
48	Pensacola, FL	2/19/2019	84	16.7
49	Ponce DeLeon, FL	2/20/2019	92	10.6
50	Quincy, FL	2/21/2019	88	10.4
51	Tennille, FL	2/22/2019	108	10.8
52	Chiefland, FL	4/11/2019	39	13.4
53	Dade City, FL	4/12/2019	92	11
54	West Frostproof, FL	4/13/2019	69	9.8
55	Moore Haven, FL	4/15/2019	80	13.5
56	Everglades, FL	4/16/2019	74	13.4
57	Homestead, FL	4/17/2019	57	14
58	Layton, FL	4/18/2019	66	12.8
59	Big Pine Key, FL	4/19/2019	36	11.7
60	Key West, FL	4/20/2019	33	10.8

Total Miles--3800

Total climb: 94,634 feet

Total descent: 94,641 feet

Roughly 330.5 hours on the bicycle

Westport, WA—5:30 AM May 27, 2017

Key West, FL—10:30 AM April 20, 2019

Heartbreaking hill—May 27, 2017 (see Chapter Nine)

Earth, Texas—February 20, 2018—Almost the halfway mark

Mayor of Earth, Texas—Jerry Carpenter—February 20, 2018

Dove Creek, Colorado September 1, 2018—69 miles of Colorado done all in one day

Megargel, TX—November 26, 2018 Me and the mayor, Paul McQueen

Officer Denny Pittman—Jena, Louisiana—February 14, 2019

Jake and Elwood, The Blues Brothers—Dunellon Florida—April 12, 2019

Sheridan Jones and me—Winter Haven, FL April 14, 2019

Randy and me with our nephews and niece, and three of their cousins—Surprise birthday party, April 14, 2019

*I'll tell you what I think of bicycling. I think it has
done more to emancipate women than any one
thing in the world. I rejoice every time I see a
woman ride by on a bike. It gives her a feeling of
self-reliance and independence the moment she
takes her seat; and away she goes, the picture of
untrammelled womanhood.*

-Susan B. Anthony—Women's Rights activist and Social
Reformer

CHAPTER 5
OLTON, TX—WINNFIELD, LA

STAGE STATS
1,920 MILES IN—1,880 TO GO
651 MILES, 9 DAYS,
AVG MPH 12.7

Planning and execution of nine days on a bicycle with
one day of rest (ten days total) while only taking five days off
work takes some doing. Fortunately, Thanksgiving and the day
after were both paid holidays at my new company. We left the
day before Thanksgiving and headed for Olton, Texas, spending
the night in the Farmington NM area, and then jumping in the
car early in the morning, arriving in Olton around 3PM. I

practically flew the 41 miles, finishing in just over 3 hours, just before dark, and I was reminded how very flat Texas is.

I showered and got some rest, and we were back on the road again to Paducah early in the morning. Fortunately we didn't have to get up at 2AM to avoid the heat, as November in Texas is pretty mild, so we would head out just at dawn.

Much of Texas was a blur. Rolling hills, but nothing substantial enough to have to walk. Lots of brown, tons of cotton bales and tiny tufts of raw cotton along the roads, with small towns every 15-20 miles. I have some friends in the Dallas area, and met my dear friend since junior high, Lisa Peters, for dinner one of the nights we were in the area. So fun to see her after a 30 year separation!

Springtown to Garland (both of them Dallas suburbs—roughly 67 miles apart) was notable. On Tuesday, November 27, 2018 I was riding through the greater Dallas, TX area. Dallas is the largest city I rode through the entire ride, with a population of 7.5 Million—4th largest metro area in the U.S. GPS was great, but one of the things about cities is you can't go as quickly as normal and you have to stop frequently for traffic lights, so despite an 8AM start, by the time I hit Garland it was after 4PM (eight hours, versus what should have taken just over six).

I had to maneuver around cars between intersections, and when I *was* able to move, I was going about 3 miles per hour—and traffic was moving even slower than I was. Each time I waited at a light I would talk to the drivers also waiting. I got various responses to my explanation of where I was going— from laughter to "Girl, you *crazy!*" But eventually the panic of more and more cars creating gridlock and jockeying for position at about 4:45 became too much, and I texted Randy and had him come get me at the nearest gas station. I didn't think they *wanted* to hit me, but I was absolutely certain that they would, despite my neon orange top and flashing lights, because it just isn't possible to pay attention to everything all at once in a high-traffic   situation. So we got up at 2AM the next day so I could finish the remaining 15 miles of that day's ride before traffic picked up.

Friday, November 30, 2018 I still had 120 miles to complete before noon on Saturday, and I was hurting badly. We got up early and got a good start, but the sky was not in our favor. The 14 counties around and east of Dallas had tornado watches in place for the previous 12 hours, continuing through the next 24. So driving back to where we had left off at the gas station just east of Marshall, TX, we revised our plan for how far Randy would be from me at any given time in case we needed quick shelter in case of emergency. He would go 5 miles ahead to start. When I passed him, he would wait about 30 minutes and drive forward 10 miles. We leap-frogged that way for 71 miles, to Ringgold, Louisiana.

I promised more details about the last 12 miles of Texas, though. All day the rain alternated about every 45 minutes between torrential and barely noticeable. The barely noticeable was pleasant enough, but I never dried off. The torrential rain was blinding. My fingers and toes were pruned when I took off my shoes and gloves.

Randy was great—he'd have me get in the car when I was resting and sit and catch my breath. It wasn't super cold, but it wasn't particularly comfortable to be drenched for nearly 7 hours. We found out after we got back to the Airbnb in Shreveport that a tornado had touched down in Harrison County, where I had started that morning. Yes, I outran a tornado. (Okay, it wasn't on the ground when I was anywhere close, but same county, same day, on a bicycle—it counts!)

December 1, 2018 we got up and I was unbelievably sore, but I had 55 miles to go, so got on and rode. My original ETA to Winnfield was around 11AM. One of my fears about leaving the bike and all my gear in storage in Louisiana was that it would rust under the intense humidity there, so I had to make sure I got it as clean as possible before storing it.

We ended up getting there just after noon, and Randy got all the other gear boxed up and organized while I cleaned, dried and polished the bike with a silicone spray and protectant lube on the chain. About an hour later we were on the road back to Utah, with the bike and gear in a storage unit in Winnfield, Louisiana and I was dead asleep.

I woke up around 3PM and immediately looked at the back of the car, as was my instinct for the last 18 months, just to make sure the bike was still with us and not causing any issues. Randy, my support and the greatest husband *ever*, reached his hand over as I gasped. "It's in the storage unit." Then, knowing my next question, clicked open his phone to show me the photo of the closed padlock. This happened several times as we made our way back across Texas and New Mexico. By the time we got into Utah on Sunday I was mostly done panicking when I would see the empty bike rack, but it was bizarre how long it took to convince my mind that it was okay to have left the bike 1,500 miles away.

It took 24 hours to drive home from Winnfield, and 26 *days* to ride the same distance (1,530 or so miles). We knew that was our last "driving" leg of the journey. I had come 651 miles that leg—the longest ride to date, in 9 riding days—leaving 1,227 miles to Key West, and 17 riding days to do them. I would have to increase my miles per day, and I wouldn't be able to ride outside during the winter in Utah to increase my stamina. I was, however, more than ⅔ finished with the miles, and the road ahead was more downhill than up, so the odds were in my favor that I would figure out a way to get them done.

PEOPLE

Of all the wonderful and incredible experiences I had during this adventure, my favorites involved the people. Police officers and random motorists would stop to check on us when we were resting for a break and water refill, just to make sure everything was okay. The loggers in Louisiana on a remote access road stopped and radioed back to the next truck to keep an eye out for me. One guy in a pickup came running back to me after we all had stopped for a funeral cortege to thank me for stopping and removing my helmet for a stranger. Two elderly gentlemen in Mississippi moseyed to the edge of the sidewalk to high-five me. In Key West the motorists, seeing that every mile starting at 10 to go I would stop and take a photo, started cheering. I already mentioned the two cyclists on the Seven

Mile bridge who passed me on the 65 foot "climb" in the middle, only to be waiting at the end, clapping and whooping like I'd just won the Tour de France. Other cyclists, restaurateurs, and Airbnb hosts cheered my progress.

In northern New Mexico I was riding on the Navajo Reservation road and was about 30 miles from anywhere. I was riding up a hill and heard the "blip" of a siren being turned on and off again quickly from behind me. The officer came on his loudspeaker and said, "Ma'am, will you pull over please?" Well, I was going between 3-4 miles per hour climbing. I was not going anywhere fast—and I still had some climb ahead of me. If I stopped before the top, I'd have to walk the rest of it. So I called back to him, "May I stop at the top? I promise I won't try and outrun you when I get there." He laughed and said that was fine.

Turns out someone driving past saw me out there, and, knowing how far the next town was, got concerned that I was going to die out there in the desert because I was lost! (I wasn't lost, and my support car was just up the road a few more miles—but they didn't know that.) They called the police because they didn't want to scare me, as I am quite obviously not Navajo, and they knew the police would take care of me if I was in a bad spot. The officer had grabbed ice, water, protein bars, and other snacks from a convenience store about 30 miles back and had them in his car just in case I was in a bad way when he got to me. I politely declined the food, but did refill my ice and water.

Probably the most memorable "anonymous" experience was when I was riding into Moab, Utah. Unbeknownst to me the Saturday I chose to ride that stretch was also the weekend leading into a very popular Jeep Safari that is older than I am. Literally tens of thousands of off-road enthusiasts descend on Moab looking for fun. Also unbeknownst to me there was a mile-and-a-half stretch of construction about a mile from the city limits where the road narrowed to two tight lanes, with a drop on the right shoulder of about 18 inches into gravel and rebar. After riding for a few hours and knowing that I was coming into town, I saw this potential disaster coming up on me fast, so I made a quick plan—I would ride just to the left of the orange barrels so long as I had no cars/jeeps coming toward me in the left lane, and when the inevitable car did come, I would stop and step down into the gravel and walk; the road was just too narrow to have two cars and a bicycle pass each other safely.

So I was riding and got about ¼ mile into the construction, and Jeeps passing me on the left. Then I could see a long line of cars and Jeeps coming toward me. I started to slow down, and I hear from behind me, "YOU GOT THIS! KEEP GOING! ALL YOU! TAKE THE WHOLE LANE! WE GOT YOU! YOU GO, GIRL!..." among other positive things. I turned and glanced behind me, to see a long line of Jeeps being held back behind me. All the young(ish) guys in the Jeep about 30 feet behind me were standing up (except the driver, of course) and using their loudspeaker to call out cheers, screaming and whistling like rabid fans.

If it took 4 minutes to make the remaining mile, I'd be shocked. But the string of jeeps passing me after the road widened and they could go faster continued honking, cheering, and treating me like I was a celebrity riding the rest of the way into Moab—roughly 10 minutes of riding. I am certain that the people who cheered quickly forgot that act of kindness. I am fairly certain that the guys who held back the mass of Jeeps wouldn't remember it today. But it is something I will never forget.

Then there are the "specific" people I met along the way. Like the mayor of Earth, Texas, population 996, named Jerry Carpenter.— I swear this man sits in the middle of the town square all day just so he can tell visitors who stop to take a picture of the "Welcome to Earth" sign that the best burger on Earth is across the street at the Wolverine Drive In. (He's not wrong, the burgers are fantastic, and the onion rings are pretty stellar as well!)

The day I finished the Utah miles we headed back to our home in Salt Lake City and celebrated at Ruth's Chris Steakhouse. The server asked if we were there for any special occasion, and we told her what we were doing. She went to the back and told the manager, Josh Cowart, what we told her. Josh came out and chatted with us for a bit, lauded how far we had come, and asked if we would be going through Mobile, Alabama—his hometown. We confirmed that yes, we were, and a few minutes later while we were eating dessert, he brought a gift card to enjoy dinner on them while we were in Mobile. The Mobile team was delightful as well, and we had a lovely meal when we got there.

Aimee Jackson is the owner of an Airbnb in Lockney, Texas. She's a gem of a human being. We stayed with her both in February and November, 2018. I rode from Olton to Lockney on Thanksgiving Day, and she had saved us all the leftovers from Thanksgiving—and what a meal! We will be friends forever, I suspect. If you ever find yourself Lockney way, tell Aimee hi from me!

Officer Denny Pittman was another find. He stopped in the Jena, Louisiana area where I had paused to refill my water and have a sandwich. We chatted for a bit about the adventure I'd been on, and I took his card. As well as being a police officer he restores VWs, has a pest control business, and Moyamoya disease—a rare, progressive cerebrovascular disorder caused by blocked arteries at the base of the brain in an area called the basal ganglia. It's a big deal. He had brain surgery a year before he met me, and had been a triathlete prior. He hadn't been on his bike since. I "friended" him on social media, because he was someone special. Denny chatted me that evening and told me more about Moyamoya and his yearning to beat it and get back to riding. I believe he will do it, if he hasn't already. Denny inspired me more than he can imagine with his resilience, strength, and love for people.

*There is no timestamp on trauma. There isn't a
formula that you can insert yourself into to get
from horror to healed. Be patient. Take up space.
Let your journey be the balm.*

-Dawn Serra, Podcaster

CHAPTER 4
AWAKENING

In the first draft of this book, this chapter didn't exist. Writing it would give potentially too much information into the darkest parts of my mind, and I didn't want to broadcast it to just anyone who had the morbid curiosity to read it. However, it too, is part of my journey, and deserves to be seen. So here goes.

In November 2018 I saw my regular doctor for some intense depression combined with panic attacks. She prescribed a very low dose of antidepressant on the condition that I also see the psychologist who was starting in the clinic in the next month or so. I agreed, and got one of her first appointments, in January 2019.

The first appointment was rough. I talked about my father's and friend's deaths, and how rough it had been. She suggested that the trauma of these was secondary to an initial trauma that happened much earlier, and her question, "When was the first time you felt abandoned?" opened up the door for six-year-old Jill to tumble into therapy, terrified that she was going to say something wrong and get whisked away by the police, with my dad not available to save her, and that nobody would ever see her again.

She explained that while this is manifesting as anxiety and depression, and though the medication helps, they are coming up again and again because it's PTSD. I wasn't processing the trauma, and *couldn't* process the trauma, because I didn't understand what had happened.

I wish I could say that knowing the root of my anxiety fixed everything, but that would be disingenuous and trite. It took several more therapy sessions and an interesting paradigm shift for me to feel like I had a handle on things.

I have long described anxiety and depression as a monster-like beast that could grab hold of me and choke the life out of me if I let it–like I was on a dark and foggy battlefield, constantly watching and waiting for the moment it would ambush me. It would be lonely and quiet, and then when anxiety did strike, the crazy *Psycho* music would play in my head, drowning all coherent thought until I lay at the bottom of a gully somewhere no one could find me, writhing in pain, shivering and whimpering, waiting for death.

It never pummeled me so hard that it actually killed me, though, so when the sun came out and the fog lifted and I was strong enough to stand up again, I would wander around feeling numb and dream of the possibility that it was the last time, that I would find my way off the foggy battlefield or be able to outrun or outride or outlast my fears the next time.

But the monster was like the Omnidroid in *The Incredibles*; it would collect data from the previous fight, go back to the lab and develop a new and improved model, and come back to fight again, repeating the cycle over and over again. It is really tough to not allow discouragement and knowledge of one's own human frailties take over when the pummelings happen so frequently. Worse, you don't get better; you live through the episodes. If you can call that "living."

From the first appointment, my psychologist would suggest to "ride the wave" of emotion instead of fighting a panic attack. That felt simple enough in the protection of a medical office, and simple enough to attempt in a setting like my living room, where I could trigger a minor panic attack by manipulating certain circumstances–which I did. She expressly stated that I should *not* try to induce a panic attack while on my coming ride in Louisiana, and I promised her I wouldn't.

But.

The day I rode out of Winnfield, Louisiana, where the "flying" miles began, I got to a small town called Jena and Google Maps had me turn off highway 84 up a little bit of a climb on State Road 772. I didn't realize that Randy had turned off bicycle directions, and had stayed on the highway into Whitehall. I was more than six miles up the hill when the road turned to dirt where county maintenance stopped. I started walking up the hill, texting him to ask how far the road was dirt.

A few moments before he got the text, he started wondering where I was and had gone to Google Maps to find my location. When he saw that I was *way* off the road he was on he got directions to me—a 15 minute drive.

I was never "alone," I was never in any *real* danger, and I was under express orders from the doctor to *not* work on my anxiety during the ride. The problem was this: I was smack-dab in the middle of Louisiana, with a bicycle, walking on a dirt road, uphill. The panic was heightened by the fact that I learned very quickly that the only vehicles that drive on that road on a regular basis are logging trucks (have you seen *City of Angels* recently? Spoiler alert—Meg Ryan gets mowed while riding a bicycle by a logging truck, and Nicholas Cage gets to live eternally without her after learning what a pear tastes like), and Louisiana outback landowners shoot guns on a frequent basis— whether just because they can, or because they're actually shooting something, I may never know. Suffice it to say, heavy-laden logging trucks coming down the hill toward me, gunshots echoing through the hills, along with the monster in my head screaming that I was going to be abandoned in the middle of nowhere and not know what to do became a perfect storm for the most memorable panic attack I'd had to date.

A panic attack is manifest by several things happening within the body and mind all at once. It is the fight; flight; freeze; and fawn reflexes, but all within your mind, and spinning out of control, feeding a myriad of effects in the body. Excess acid is dumped into the stomach, sometimes causing vomiting; the mind can become hyper-vigilant or overly muddy; the heart races or slows dramatically, causing dizziness, blurred vision, and sometimes loss of consciousness; the capillaries constrict, sometimes causing tingling in the toes and fingers as well as migraines. The body doesn't quite know what to do or when, especially if none of the instinctive moves are unavailable or don't work.

I remember being on that road and believing for certain that the time on that hill was the last few minutes of my life. Something on that mountain would kill me, for sure. It is interesting how the mind will tell you absolutely bold-faced lies in order to protect itself. I heard the tell-tale sound of a lumber truck turning the corner onto the road and saw it barreling toward me, the driver riding the air brakes as he saw a random girl walking up the hill toward him wearing neon pink and pushing a bicycle. He stopped right beside me and asked if I was lost.

"Nah, my husband is coming. I just got on the wrong road. Thanks, though!"

"Do you have enough water? Do you need anything? I got some water bottles up here."

"I'm good," I lied. Sure, I had enough water. But I was *dying* out there in backwood Louisiana, long before Randy got to me.

"Okay! Good luck, little lady!"

Over the course of the next 14 ½ minutes or so a similar exchange happened eight or nine times. A truck would turn onto the road, at least slow down enough to confirm that I was still okay, and more often they would offer me water and/or snacks from their lunch boxes, I would say I was fine, and keep walking. For a moment after each truck passed, I believed I was fine, like I said I was, and then the panic started to hit me again as the monster whispered in my ear, "Randy may be on his way, but he won't find you. He will never find you." Yeah, the monster could be pretty mean. For that moment, though, the monster would seem quieter as the sound and smell of the diesel engines rolled down the hill.

When Randy did arrive, the panic attack was over. I had survived a "big one", grateful that it hadn't lasted longer than it had, and I had "ridden the wave" like a pro.

Several times during the following week the monster would try and scream at me, and I would feel like I could smack it down with a solid, "Look, Randy is never leaving me out here alone, so you can go climb in a hole and leave me alone. I've got things to do and places to go." But the monster, as it walked toward the hole, would always leave me with a parting comment, "What if he doesn't have a choice?", and a mini panic attack would happen, because the monster was right—we all are going to die sometime, and today could be the day just as easily for Randy as it was for my dad in 2004.

Each time the monster would ask, she got more power, and every time we separated for another 15-20 mile ride, I got the opportunity to worry for an hour. What if Randy got mowed by a big rig and I found him first? What if he drove off a cliff? (the answer to that one was literally laughing out loud, looking around—there are no cliffs to speak of in this section of the world!) What if he had a heart attack and I could have saved him with CPR but I'm not there? What if it's "his time"?

By Thursday, February 21, I had reached the conclusion that *even if* the worst thing my monster could come up with actually happened, I wouldn't need to decide by myself what to do. *Someone* would help me figure out what to do first. *Someone* would help.

It's not quite as simple as the advice Mister Rogers gave to preschoolers, "Look for the helpers", but the concept is highly relevant. If you need help and cannot process or decide what to do for yourself, *ask for help*. We tend to think because we became adults we can and *should* help and do things for ourselves. For the most part, we are right. We *can* do it for ourselves. We *should* take care of ourselves and those for whom we have accepted responsibility (spouse, children, pets). But we don't have to do those things alone. We have our "people"—even if they are strangers—to help us. Please know that no matter how old or young you are, you can look to your people, your "helpers" for those days.

Also, when you can, *be* a "helper." Don't think that because you aren't a police officer or firefighter, doctor, nurse, or EMT that you cannot help people in distress. Be a "noticer." Notice when people are late to work who normally aren't. Notice when they aren't there at all. Notice people on the side of the road with or without their flashers on. Notice when someone comes to church who normally doesn't. Notice when someone is struggling for the door—or notice when someone is 25 feet behind you. Are you *really* too busy to hold the door an extra four seconds, make eye contact, and say good morning?

The smallest action can turn around someone's day, and if everyone got into the habit of noticing their surroundings and the people they are with, I believe it would relieve many burdens of life—not just those of the people you help, but your own. When you are busy noticing others' moments of pain—even if it is just enough to send a silent prayer of recovery to whomever an ambulance is going to pick up—you notice your own less. You are more grateful that you came home at your normal time, to an intact home, and a family who loves you. You are happy to see your spouse, your kids, and yes, even the blasted dog messes in the backyard.

My next visit after returning home, I recounted the episode on the hill, and felt pretty proud of myself, having battled the monster and won–though to be precise, I had held it at bay, at best.

But then the psychologist said that phrase, "ride the wave," again, and something clicked in my brain. I was *never* going to be able to beat the monster, because the monster was *in* my brain. In a split second that familiar "mic drop" feedback hit me sitting in the doctor's office again—feedback that said, "NO WONDER NOTHING IS WORKING! I am hardwired to fight this monster, and the monster is ME!" Cue the playing of *The Incredibles* scene where Mr. Incredible jumps into the Omnidroid and the programming unwittingly destroys itself, piece by piece.

But wait, she's still talking. I set that piece aside for a moment and heard the momentary echo of what she said. "Ride the wave." In a bad 80's movie they would have slowed down time and taken a close-up shot of her lips as the doctor said it again: "RRRRRRIIIIIIIIIIIIDDDDDDDDDDE TTTTTHHHHHHHUUUUUUHHHHHH WAAAAAAAAAAAAAAAAAAYYYYYYYYYYYYYYVVVVVVV VVVVVVVE."

I stopped the psychologist—fairly abruptly, but not in an attempt to be rude or argumentative; I was having a breakthrough thought, and I couldn't complete it without her stopping.

In the silent 45 seconds or so, I sat the monster piece of my mind down in the corner and repeated, "Ride the wave," like that was the first time I'd ever heard it in my life. The monster was pouting in the corner. "Ride the wave," I whispered. She nodded.

The next 5 minutes or so were a bit of a blur as words tumbled out of my mouth talking as quickly as I could think them. Maybe my anxiety didn't have anything to *do* with a monster—the monster is just the part of me that's afraid that I'm not good enough, or strong enough, or brave enough, or smart enough, or fast enough, or old enough, or young enough, or thin enough, or pretty enough, or "tom-boy" enough, or feminine enough, or femin*ist* enough, or "Mormon" enough, or conservative enough, or liberal enough, or "mom" enough, or wife enough, or happy enough, or loved enough, or motivated enough, or energetic enough, or, well, just plain *ENOUGH* enough. Maybe all I needed to do was reframe the picture. I had always pictured this monster and me fighting in a field, and the monster always being better than I would be, no matter how good I got. But using her "wave", I needed to picture myself— one and whole—in a boat on the ocean.

Waves are waves. They are not designed to outlast, outwit, or outplay you. They are literally a method of conveying energy. Sometimes we get into situations we cannot—and should not—even attempt to travel alone. It's too much of a climb, too rough a road, too much or too dangerous weather. Sure, there are waves that can capsize a boat in dramatic fashion, especially if the captain of the boat isn't seasoned, but a captain who knows the sea can harness the energy and use it to their best use if they don't try to fight them. If the waves are too big for my skills, I can recognize that I don't *have* to do it on my own. I can call someone who loves me. I can ask the nearest stranger. Again, someone will be happy to help me. And if, in the rare event that I am out "at sea" completely alone when the really big waves hit, I still have God to call on. He may not stop the wind or the waves. But He can quiet *me*, and that can be enough.

In that moment, I got a glimpse of peace I hadn't seen in years. The monster was silent as the most calming feeling passed through me. For that moment, I believed the monster was dead, and I wouldn't have to fight her anymore. That night, however, I had another think coming. I slept fitfully for a few short hours, and had a dream.

In my dream I was in a brightly lit field that I recognized as the battlefield of anxiety on which I had fought for so long. The sun was warm, but not hot, and because I could still smell the dew in the air I knew it was about half an hour or so after dawn. I could hear harmless morning insects buzzing around and just felt happy and peaceful there. Suddenly I heard the shrieking sound of something dying, and I whirled around to see a dilapidated shed-like structure that looked like it might fall over at any moment. I ran toward it to find "my" monster, shriveling and wilting before me in the corner (think Wicked Witch of the West after Dorothy threw the water). As I took a few more steps into the space, she changed before my eyes into my six-year-old self, crying, shivering, and terribly, terribly afraid.

I put my arm carefully around her and told her I wouldn't let her die—not ever—but I she also didn't have to take care of *me* anymore. I would take care of her. She cried some more, and I held her tightly. When I felt her relax, I pulled away and held her chin, directing her eyes toward mine and said, "I am sorry. I didn't understand that you were trying to protect me and that you were so afraid. You are *not* a monster, and I love you. How about we go take a ride on a boat? There's nothing to be afraid of, but if you do get afraid, you've got me, and I've got you. Let's go live out our world of possibilities."

I took her hand and stood, and she tentatively stood and walked with me out of the shed toward the shoreline, where a boat sat waiting. We stepped aboard, me taking strength from her trust and her trusting my strength, and both of us looking toward the horizon, we started to untie the ropes holding us to the dock… and I woke up.

I tell you this dream and my experience with the psychologist not because I believe it "fixed" my problem. I still feel waves of anxiety and depression often. I still have difficult, sometimes physically painful moments where I hate everything and get frustrated and angry with myself, and believe that I have never been, and will never be enough to match the severity of the storms I will face. I feel small and weak and afraid. Instead of Fight, Flight, Freeze, or Fawn, I Pause, Ponder, Pray, and Press on, but changing the framework of the issue *did not change the issue* any more than changing the frame of the Mona Lisa changes her mysterious smile.

But I also know that the waves aren't there to challenge me or kill me or learn from my patterns *how* best to kill me. They are there because I choose to be at sea, and I get to choose to be at sea or not to be at sea every day that I'm alive. When I know there is a storm coming, I don't have to choose to go to sea. I can make wise choices, with counsel from my friends or people I trust, who can predict unfavorable conditions, and then I can choose another day to sail. Nobody is asking me to walk on the waves. Nobody would dream of it. All I am expected to do is get in my boat, learn from the conditions of the day, and become better.

Give a man a fish and feed him for a day. Teach a man to fish and feed him for a lifetime. Teach a man to cycle and he will realize fishing is stupid and boring.

– Archbishop Desmond Tutu

CHAPTER 3
LOUISIANA, MISSISSIPPI, ALABAMA, AND INTO FLORIDA

STAGE STATS
2,489 MILES IN — 1,311 TO GO
660 MILES, 8 DAYS,
AVG MPH 11.4

In the video compilation of drone footage assembled by my son d'Artagnan there is a "scene" of me riding across a bridge. (search YouTube for Jypsy Jill Rides to view) The sky is reflected in the water, and the water is so placid it looks like I'm riding on a bridge over a mirror. That is pretty indicative of my Louisiana experience after that first super rainy day. Louisiana is green, green, green, with a lot of mud and mosquitos thrown in just to keep you grounded. (Brad, I'm not dissing on Louisiana, I'm just saying the mud and mosquitos are a biological hazard for cyclists.)

Quick physics lesson. When we lived in Australia someone explained why all the greens seemed more vibrant and alive. The simple explanation is humidity, but the more involved explanation is not what you'd normally think: prisms. Yes, the dampness pulls some of the dust we have in the west down and into the soil, making the plants greener and stronger, but even more than that, the more humid it is, the more water particles you are actually seeing through. Thus the more water particles in the air there are, the more light is brought into your eye from different angles, filling your eye with more light, and the more your eye is able to process color. Yep. The more you know!

We flew into Alexandria, Louisiana late on February 13th. Valentine's day morning we got up and got our rental car, and drove to Winnfield. I was on the bike by 10:15 with a lofty goal in mind of 89 miles to Natchez, MS, but only made 63 before I was exhausted and the day was pretty well spent. Not to worry, though—the "must do" mileage was 59, so I was still on track to get to my original planned stopping point of Tennille, FL.

Crossing the bridge over the Mississippi was barely even a challenge on day two (riding day 43), but as soon as I was out of Louisiana, I learned *very* quickly that I was not in the west anymore. My straight, blonde hair and #Even-Paler-Than-Normal-Because-It's-Winter-Where-I-Live skin was glaring evidence that I was not only in the racial minority—but I also saw almost no women! I wasn't afraid, but it sure felt like I was conspicuous as I rode through neighborhoods and towns that visually at least, seemed populated almost solely with African American men.

Everyone was very kind and cordial, if they said or did anything at all, and I got some interesting looks and double-takes as I passed through the main thoroughfares and neighborhoods. The spaces between the towns were lush and green, with a few houses spattered across the countryside. When I would stop for breaks or we were driving to our planned stay for the night we wondered aloud what people who live out in the sticks like this *do* for a living? We still don't know for sure, but there do seem to be a lot of people living nowhere near other people or towns where they might be employed. Maybe they're the people selling cool stuff on Etsy. You can't prove otherwise by me, for sure.

At a small town called Prentiss, MS (population 960 in 2017), a quick pit stop gave me another one of my favorite human encounters—I stopped at a gas station to use the restroom, and when I walked in a UPS driver chewing the fat with the cashier at the register said, "GIRL! HOW FAR YOU GOING? I'VE BEEN LEAPFROGGING YOU SINCE LUCIEN!" I told him Hattiesburg, and he squinted at me and said, "Don't tell my supervisor. He'll put me on a bike and make me take a bigger route!" We all laughed.

At the other end of town my Google directions turned me onto a trail called Longleaf Trace. In our experience in Louisiana, trails could get sketchy as to reliability—sometimes they would be paved for 10-15 feet and then mud, and other times they would look like the remnants of a Monster Truck Mud Rally with no evidence that a trail had ever existed. In any event, trails made me nervous, so Randy would scout as far as he could to see if I was likely to need to backtrack when the trail got ugly. So when Randy had texted to tell me he couldn't follow it very far, but that the road crossed several places where it *looked* like it was a pretty decently paved trail that I would love, I got a little excited. He was right.

Longleaf Trace is one of the completed portions of the planned 4,000 mile bicycle trail across America. (see https://www.railstotrails.org/ for more information.) The premise is that the smaller railroads which were once interconnected but are no longer in use are removing the ties, tracks, and other hazards and replacing them with pavement. Maintenance will be done by the individual states. Mississippi did this back in 2000 in several places, and from the Prentiss area to just south of Hattiesburg there are forty-four gloriously flat and shady miles. They felt like a reward for having come every inch of over 2,750 miles and climbed more than 66,000 feet.

Between towns (nationwide—not just in the south, though it was more pronounced in the south) it is easy to focus just on riding and not notice things like local culture or socio-economic demographics. When I got into Hattiesburg, the fact that I am Caucasian, blonde, and female stuck out like a pregnant pole-vaulter. African-American men of all ages would drive by very slowly and I could tell they were concerned about why I might be there. When I got to the dead-center of town, a man in his early 20s rode up next to me on a bicycle with a do-rag on his head, no shirt, flip flops, and basketball shorts that were probably three sizes too big.

"Girl, you ain't from here."

"No, sir, that's for sure, I am not."

"Where'd you come from?"

"Well, yesterday I started my day in Lucien, but I started riding a couple years ago in Washington State and have ridden all the miles between the Seattle area and here."

(Shocked look—and then the unexpected question) "What made you choose Hattisburg?" (spelling changed to match his pronunciation)

I chuckled a little, because while the shocked look was expected, I didn't have a ready answer for that one. While I remembered I was in the Bible belt and should come up with something that helped him know that I meant nobody any harm or offense, I ultimately decided that the truth would be my best bet on appealing to a common sensibility. "Well, when I wake up in the morning and get ready to ride, I ask God to keep me safe and to meet the kindest people along the way, and Google for exact directions, and between the two of them, I've always found the right way."

He laughed at that, but spent a few seconds processing what I had said before commenting, "God and Google. Huh. Yes, ma'am, you sure did."

We chatted for a little bit longer as we rode through town, and he wished me a safe and blessed (they use that word a *lot* in the South—I want to use it more!) ride, and we went our separate ways.

I don't always feel like I have had visible angels ride alongside me, but that day in Hattiesburg Mississippi, I knew that I had been guided and guarded by an angel as I rode through a little bit of a sketchy part of town.

Just past Hattiesburg I looked at my tracker and discovered that I had 999 miles left to get to Key West. For 2,801 miles I'd had four digits ahead of me and suddenly I had three. I sat down on the side of the road and had myself a cry. I was almost 74% finished and it *just* occurred to me that it might indeed be possible to complete this thing. Within the next second I knew that there was nothing on earth that would *stop* me from finishing. That's heady stuff when you've been thinking about a project for almost 10 years and *actively* pursuing it for 630 days—with fewer than 65 calendar days and only 14 riding days until it would be complete.

The next day we stayed in Mobile, Alabama, and our Airbnb host (hi, James!) suggested that I might want to avoid Pritchard—which was directly where the Google map had intended for me to ride—as it has an extremely high crime rate. His statement reminded me of a conversation I'd had with a friend who had served a mission in the area, and Josh had *also* specifically warned me to avoid Pritchard. According to Google, "looking at violent crime specifically, Prichard, AL has a violent crime rate that is 248% higher than the Alabama average and 377% higher than the national average." So yes, we decided to avoid Pritchard. Thank you James, Josh, Google and God, for continuing to keep me safe and sending angels along my path.

I still wanted to finish all the miles I'd intended for Alabama, so I rode south instead of east from Mobile. The first two hours was pounding rain, but as soon as we got on the ferry to Dauphin Island, it was just windy. When we got to Pensacola, Florida I had 844 miles left of the ride. The ride between Dauphin Island and Pensacola was windy, but bearable, and gave me a taste of the bridges between islands I would get again in the Keys.

ANIMALS

Since there were more (and more "exotic" than the west) animals east of Albuquerque, this seems like a good place to talk about animals. Not that there weren't plenty of animals in the west, but I'm fairly used to seeing them on the road out here, so raccoons, deer, elk, moose, dogs, cows, goats, horses, rattlesnakes, lizards, rabbits, tarantulas, squirrels, coyotes, skunks, eagles, and 1,000 other types of birds were regular occurrences. Okay, to be fair, the moose was twice, not regular. I even saw a porcupine in Washington and beavers in Oregon.

Most of the animals in the west I had a pretty good feel for—if you don't bug them, they won't bug you, at least most of the time. When I got into New Mexico scorpions started to appear pretty regularly, but they got much bigger and more prevalent in Texas. Also armadillos—which were in New Mexico as well, but I only ever saw carcasses in New Mexico, whereas Texas in the early mornings I could see them crossing the road 25 or so feet ahead of me. They are very cautious, but their eyes shine in the headlights, you just have to watch for them.

Not quite to Louisiana, but east of Dallas, early in the morning I was riding along and humming to myself. Suddenly I heard a rustling of the tall wild grass to my right, and I saw a flash of black fur, about 10 feet away from me. I had startled a feral hog (aka wild boar) and the race was on. He was running the same direction I was riding, and I couldn't tell if he was on my side of the barbed-wire fence or the other side. I believed I might be in trouble either way as my adrenaline kicked in and I went faster, and he, seeing me speed up, ran even faster. His tusks curled almost to his ears, and I was very concerned. I decided to give him some space, since I then knew I couldn't outrun him, and see what he would do. As soon as I backed off he veered right, and then I could see that he was on the other side of the fence, but I believe he was heavier than I am, and he was terrifying, as I don't know the nature of feral hogs and if they will charge without cause.

Another time in Louisiana I heard a low, soft and short "grrr" come from across someone's yard as I rode past. Most dogs bark their heads off and I yell and they go away. I knew this grey pit bull wasn't into warning barks, he was out for blood. I kicked it into as fast as I could go without a downhill lead, and looked at my speedometer on my watch—22 mph. So I backed off a little on speed to conserve some energy, since it was still early on in the ride that day. When I looked back he was a little farther behind me, but still coming. He chased me for a full mile at 18.7 miles per hour, and never barked. Other than that encounter, the dogs were just loud and not so much scary as funny. Most of the dogs would bark their heads off and chase me for a hundred yards or so. As soon as I yelled, "GO HOME!" they would usually back off.

The most rattlesnakes I saw in one day was nine, just northeast of Mountain Home, Idaho. The original post office of Mountain Home was at a stagecoach stop called Rattlesnake Station, and in roughly the same geographical location as my route, so that seemed appropriate.

There was the bull elk (Oregon) that may as well have been a dairy cow as much as he paid attention to me. He just stood by the side of the road and watched as I rode by. The porcupine was pretty nervous about me, probably because he couldn't hear me on my bike as I flew by on a downhill stretch. Countless deer, in every state (except Georgia, only because I really wasn't in Georgia long enough) I rode. Some of the most beautiful horses I've ever seen, too, scattered across the countryside.

The birds varied from as small as the hummingbirds that I could almost not see they were buzzing so fast, but would catch glimpses of sometimes, to the enormous turkey vultures that seemed to hang out waiting for me to fall over. They reminded me of the vultures in Disney's Robin Hood. I could almost hear Nutsy saying, "One o'clock, and all's well!" as I saw them sitting on telephone poles above me. There were some pretty huge birds in Florida as well, but I don't know what kind of birds they were, some kind of crane or pelican or something. They would graze the ocean in the Keys and I could hear them sometimes.

The Alabama miles were all done by Tuesday of that week. I had three more days of riding to get to Tennille, Florida—a hefty 288 miles from Pensacola, and a total of 667 miles, and with only eight days to do them in (16 more miles than my previous longest stretch, in one fewer day) if I wanted to be done in time to get the bike serviced before storing it for 45 days.

Pensacola Naval Base is where the world-famous Blue Angels train. As I was close-by my music wasn't loud enough to hear over the roar of jet engines—the sound I very affectionately called, "The Sound of Freedom." I was in tears as that roar was louder and softer for the next hour or so. I didn't see them as often as I heard them, but the Blue Angels are a favorite, and what a lovely reminder of my youth spent on military bases.

Wednesday and Thursday were spent riding across the panhandle of Florida. Hurricane Michael had come through about three months prior, and the people were still struggling to recover. The landscape will forever be changed in places where the winds sheared off trees—it looked like a giant swather had gone through and removed all the leaves and lopped off the top 15-30 feet of trees that had stood for decades. There were mobile homes that were literally upside down, and ceiling fans with light kit and intact light bulbs more than a mile away from the nearest house just sitting on the side of the road.

I was talking with a guy about the devastation I had seen and he explained how the entire ecosystem was redefined when those trees were killed. There are bugs in the area that only eat dead wood. When the trees die, especially all at once, the bugs are able to reproduce quickly and devour the trees. When this happens, rodents and feral hog population explodes, eating and foraging everything in their path. If the EPA didn't come in and help the families who owned the land with the trees, their entire property could be under wetland and swamps within 6-8 months. They are given farm equipment and pesticides and taught how to grow new crops to control the erosion and parasitic animal population. So when you see on the news that a hurricane has caused *billions* of dollars ($25.1Billion in Michael's case) in damages, they aren't talking just lost shingles and broken windows and flood damage. They're talking entire livelihoods for some families. They're talking about trying to hold back a wave of domino effects that will affect the ecosystem *forever*.

On Friday morning I started riding in a small town called Quincy northwest of Tallahassee, at 4:00AM with my goal of completing 114 miles to Tennille, Florida; my longest ride ever. Ninety percent of the miles were flat, so I anticipated a simple, albeit long, ride. The road through Tallahassee and south beyond there was a beautiful ride, with slightly overcast temps in the mid-sixties. Then at noon the sun came out and the temperature shot up to the mid-seventies, and it was 83 before 1PM as I got to roughly the Perry area. With 28 or so miles to go, it was full sun, 80+ degrees outside, and I'd been riding for 8 ½ hours even with the breaks I'd take (I'd been monitoring them so I only stopped for 10 minutes at the most). My energy was waning, and I didn't believe I had another 30 miles in me with the heat, humidity, and full sun. At one of the stops Randy doused me with sunscreen and I soldiered on, but as overheated as I kept getting, I had a water bottle that I kept spraying on my arms and legs, even though I knew I was rinsing off the sunscreen and causing myself more problems long-term.

By the time I had 15 miles left for the day the only thing working properly was the bicycle. I was dizzy, overheated, and it was 90 degrees. Salty drops of sweat and sunscreen dripped into my eyes and cracked my lips. My lip was bleeding from a previous crack, and kept dripping fresh blood onto my shirt. My recovery drink tasted like bile, so I refilled my water bottles with as much ice as I could get into them and regular water. All the food I had been eating for several days in a row now sounded awful, so Randy got me some grilled chicken strips at a convenience store. The taste of the seasoning was nauseating, so I tore off the edges and only ate the more bland meat inside. My feet felt like I was stepping onto a flaming hot grill with every revolution. I was spitting and coughing about every hundred yards because my body was creating so much mucus (a serious sign of dehydration). I would see dead animals on the side of the road and *swear* they were moving. It was bad, to be honest, but I couldn't stop. I had to keep going until I got to Tennille.

And then, what felt like all-of-a-sudden, I was in the car and Randy was driving. I wiped my face and caught my breath and called the place in Tallahassee where they had told me they could get my bike in for service, and the service manager answered. Well, the person who said they could do it in 24 hours wasn't there, and nobody had forwarded the message, but the service manager by a coincidental miracle was going to be to work on Saturday, and would take care of it himself. If I hadn't called in having completed the ride that day, I wouldn't have been able to have the bike serviced at all before leaving for Utah, and that could have been a very bad thing. 667 devilish miles in eight riding days, and I had 546 miles to go to Key West.

We met Dawn and her boyfriend (at the time) Freddy in Tallahassee, and went to dinner on Friday night. They had brought down Freddy's truck and volunteered to take all my gear and store it for the 45 days between then and when we came back to complete Florida, as Tallahassee is only a two hour drive from Leesburg, where Dawn was living now. They also offered to take us to Saint George Island, since it had been reopened after the hurricane in the past week, and we accepted both offers.

We learned a little more about the devastation on our trip through the area. There was some debate locally about whether Saint George Island, which was all but completely demolished, would even be able to open again. We stopped at a local restaurant that had only outdoor tables and there were ceiling fans that didn't have any blades on them as well as ceiling fans that were working and some that were just the posts coming out of the ceiling. They had not been stocked with all their regular menu items, so we didn't stay for lunch, but seeing how they were still reeling from the impact was tough. I admire their tenacity and strength, and took heart from their experience, as well as sending my prayers that their recovery would be simpler than it seemed from my point of view.

The next week or so, Dawn and Freddy got engaged and asked Randy to perform the wedding when we would be there to complete the ride. Randy got an internet license to perform the wedding, and we booked our flight to Atlanta, instead of Tallahassee, so we could pick up the bike on our way through instead of Dawn and Freddy having to make another trip on our behalf.

MAINTENANCE AND SELF-CARE

All told, I went through 13 tires, three chains, two sets of brake and derailleur cables, 10 bottles of chain lube, 6 tubes of chamois butter, approximately 40 gallons of water, countless hydration tablets, bowls of oatmeal, and peanut butter sandwiches. I could have gone through many more tubes, had I not gone tubeless, but on the advice of my amazing friend and the American Fork Trek store, Kris Nolte, dodged that bullet. I also saw (estimate) 7 doctors, 10 chiropractors, 3 physical therapists, a psychologist, a couple of massage therapists, and countless friends who helped me with the mental aspect.

My point is this: I took really good care of my bike. But I neglected to take care of me until I was injured; emotionally, physically, spiritually or mentally. I would ride any hour of the day or night, eat whatever sounded good either on-route or while I wasn't riding, and take care of my body and skin only when I'd overdone it with sun, friction, too much or too little nutrition. I didn't get enough sleep or rest, and it took its toll on my body.

Toward the end of the ride people started asking, "So, what's next?", and I would always come back with either an, "I don't know," or, "What, 3,800 miles isn't enough?", or "Randy gets veto rights on anything I think I want to try, so ask him."

When we were driving to Key West to pick my mom up from the airport there the day before I finished, Randy and I were talking about the ride and my answer to that question, and he suggested that I learn "the art of self-care."

I considered that for some time, including while I was on the bike the next day, flying home, and beginning my "new life", post-ride. I asked for people's ideas on what they do for self-care. I thought to make a schedule of things that I do to take care of my body on a regular basis like spa treatments, pedicures, manicures, and all that kind of thing.

Yes, self-care can be all those things, but I kept thinking there must be more to it than that. So I searched for "self-care" on Amazon and found a book called, "Bare", by Susan Hyatt. Susan is a master certified life coach and a powerhouse speaker. I got the physical book, and loved it so much I got it on Audible as well. She discusses self-care in a vastly different way than it had ever occurred to me—she asks herself, "What feels like love?" whenever she has a decision to make—whether that's what she wants to eat, how much she wants to eat, what she wants to do in her business, in her personal life, in her parenting, exercise, anything. What feels like love?

I'm working on it. I've been working on it for three months. I find that it's easier to consider what feels like love when I am not distracted, stressed, afraid, or upset about something; when I am still and gentle with myself I know that I am showing love to myself. So far the most interesting thing about it is that I find that I also ask myself what would feel like love right now for the people in my life? What would help Randy know how much I love him today? What would help the checker at the grocery store know how much I appreciate their work today? What would help a friend who posted about a personal struggle know that I love them and am willing to share their burden today? To whom would God want me to reach out today? What loving message may I convey?

It is an art and not a science. There is no perfect formula for this type of self-care. The simplicity of asking that question occasionally gets mired down in the "have-to" of daily tasks and priorities, but I truly believe that soon—very soon, I hope—love will be the instinctive number one priority.

And if you are at home, and you're sitting on your couch and you're watching this right now, all I have to say is that this is hard work. I've worked hard for a long time, and it's not about, you know...it's not about winning. But what it's about is not giving up. If you have a dream, fight for it. There's a discipline for passion. And it's not about how many times you get rejected or you fall down or you're beaten up. It's about how many times you stand up and are brave and you keep on going.

-Lady Gaga, at the Oscars, Feb 24,2019

CHAPTER 2
TENNILLE TO KEY WEST, FL

STAGE STATS
3,254 MILES IN — 546 TO GO, 8
RIDING DAYS
AVG MPH 12.3

We flew into Atlanta, GA instead of Tallahassee, drove to Leesburg late April 10, gathered all the gear and the bicycle, and were on our way to Tennille, FL relatively early in the morning on April 11. At noon we picked up groceries at Walmart in Perry, Florida and it was approximately 85 degrees, with the projected high at around 98. While driving, we discussed the options—I could ride in the middle of the day, and possibly cripple the remaining days by overheating or getting dehydrated, or we could wait until it started to cool off around 5:30 and gently warm into 8 days of riding while it was cool. We decided that was the best option, checked into our Airbnb early, and took a nap.

April 11, 2019—Riding day number 52 –
Tennille to Chiefland
39 miles, 507 to go

We got back to Tennille at 5:30, unloaded the bike and everything I needed, and I was riding by 5:40. Sunset in Florida was at 7:48, and I estimated I'd be 3 hours and 12 minutes based on two mph faster than my average, since it is quite flat. So I would be an hour in the dark, regardless, but I'd been challenging myself to beat the estimated time, so I set under three hours as the goal.

At Cross City I grabbed more water and got onto a beautiful trail. Covered by trees and apart from the road, I could pick up some speed confidently and wasn't getting too hot. With 12 miles left I was projected to finish at 2 hours 52 minutes, and I was thrilled, but I was still going to be riding in the dark for 48 minutes. I said a quick prayer that I'd be able to see well enough or that I'd know when to make my way to the road and have Randy follow me.

Back up a bit—roughly around the halfway mark, I started a tradition that before I ride each day I'd pray that I'd be safe, that I would be up to the challenge of the day, and that sometime during the ride I would know that I was being watched over by loved ones who have passed on.

Three miles later the sun was down and I started to get more than a little nervous. My eyes hadn't adjusted to the waning light, and my headlight wasn't strong enough to get past 15—20 feet out.

Then the miracle occurred. Okay. Miracle may be just a hair of a stretch. But it felt like a miracle.

In Utah and most of the west we don't have fireflies. I often forget they exist. But as it got darker and I got more nervous, the Florida landscape began to flash. Not "real" light— I couldn't see better because of it, but the tiny insects are eating the plants on the side of the trail, and because of the million flashes on the side of the trail, I could keep riding into the darkness. Now please don't judge my music—I have a pretty diverse selection on these playlists. But I was riding along with the beautiful flashes of light and the Lady Gaga song, "Applause" came on, and suddenly the flashing lights were paparazzi in my head, each an adoring fan from beyond the grave shouting out cheers and taking photos.

I knew it was just nature. I knew it was just bugs. But for a moment I felt like my friends in heaven were able to send me a message—"we're all watching and cheering you on."

April 12—Riding day number 53—
Chiefland—Dade City
92 miles, 415 to go.

The good news about Florida south of the panhandle is it's flat. The bad news is that it's *super* flat; the kind of flat that reminded me that riding a bike 92 miles is hard work—arduous and tedious. I had planned out my time, adding an hour for leeway, and created playlists for every day that had no repeats for songs. There were lots of animals, and the wildlife kept me smiling as they'd scamper across the road or beside me as I surprised them. Rabbits, foxes, turtles, armadillo, and birds were my companions throughout the early morning and day. I wasn't sore yet, since it was only day two, but I felt the heat substantially more than I'd anticipated. When we left Utah it was snowing. Locally it was 80+ degrees with high humidity, and it was taking its toll on me. I rode 73 miles and was exhausted, so went to the Airbnb and took a long nap, then got back up and rode again late that night with Randy following me in the dark. I did see a small alligator on the side of the road, finally, so that felt like I was in Florida.

April 13—Riding day number 54 –
Dade City—West Frostproof
69 miles, 346 to go.

From my blog that day: Man, it's hot. Only got 60 of the 68 miles planned in, and it took much longer than expected. I fear I've bitten off more than I can chew, not planning for the heat. I finished the last 8 miles in the wee hours of Sunday when it had cooled down, but the plan will have to change to ride most of them in the dark if I'm going to finish the race against the sun.

From my memory: I was nervous that Sunday morning after I finished the last 8 miles before daylight. Feeling like you have one shot at the last 346 miles, and having 6 riding days to do them in is intimidating at best. Randy had asked if he could "have" Sunday afternoon where I didn't make plans with friends in Florida, so I did that, but went to an early lunch with my friend Sheridan. He picked me back up and headed to Orlando. We pulled into the Worldmark resort in Orlando and I learned that Jon and Amanda were there. (Randy's brother and his wife) I was super excited to see them, and was *shocked* when I knocked on the door and learned (with eight screaming children) that they also had their five kids with them, and were visiting Amanda's brother Aaron and his wife Lindsey who lives there with their kids. They had a surprise birthday party for me, complete with cake, lasagna, streamers, a banner, noise makers, hats, and as my mom would call it, the whole shebang. We enjoyed a few hours of relaxation and chatting about the ride and their Spring Break vacation.

At the end of the visit the kids went outside to have an Easter Egg hunt (since Easter was the following week, on my birthday), and Jon and Randy and I hung back preparing to head back to our Airbnb. I asked Randy if he and Jon would pray with me, since I was super concerned about the aches and pains I was feeling and how hot I had been. They of course were willing and able to do so, and asked a sweet blessing of peace, strength, and comfort on me. I slept in the van on the way back, and when we got home, slept again pretty well.

April 15—Riding day number 55 –
West Frostproof—Moore Haven
80 miles, 266 to go.

With 80 miles planned, we were out of the Airbnb by 2:30AM and riding by 3:30. For comparison's sake I have directly copied the blog entry for April 15.

3:30 AM is dark. Betcha didn't know that.

The initial mile felt slow and tired. But I settled in, knowing it was going to be a long day, and my last 70+ day on route.

Picked up speed a little on a slight downhill grade, and my legs got warmed up. The music was pumping and I just kept going.

Looking at the GPS I wanted to be at the first stop by 4:45 AM, shaving 4 minutes off the projected time. I made it with one minute to spare. Took a five minute break and got more fuel and was back at it.

Checked the GPS and projected time for 37 miles (the next stop) was 6:28. So I set another goal—40 by 6:30. Which I didn't make. It was 6:31. Grabbed some water and hard boiled eggs and was back on the road even quicker. Halfway done before sunrise is great, but once the sun gets up all bets are off as to how far I could get before I hit diminishing returns.

At 50 miles in I had been on the bike under 4 hours and still feeling strong. Not sure where the energy came from, but my legs were feeling pretty solid.

At the 56 mile break I told Randy I wanted to be done by 10 AM and jumped back on the bike with an ETA of 10:02 and restarted my watch.

At the 58 mile mark I looked at my watch and noticed that I was just over 4 hours and 30 minutes. Could I cut the 10 AM ETA even more by aiming for under six hours? No reason not to try, so I dug deep and pushed a hair harder.

The 60-65 mile split was exhilarating. Coming in under 20 minutes when you've been on a bike for five hours (for me) was unbelievable. It was evident that it might be close, but I would definitely be under six hours.

I wish I'd had a camera going when I got to the car. I'd told Randy I wanted to be done by 10, and it was 9:38. The final time on the bike was 5:48. My speed was not quite 14 miles per hour, sustained for almost six full hours.

In my ride postmortem I do in my head I tried to figure out what just happened, and the only thing I can figure is this: I got enough rest, I had prayed with my husband, and I focused EARLY on staying hydrated and not allowing for dehydration to creep in.

Today's ride is a game changer I think.

April 16—Riding day number 56 –
Moore Haven—Everglades Airboat Excursions
74 miles, 192 to go.

We got a good early start, but the cycling directions wanted me to take a completely dark trail that Randy couldn't scout, and I didn't know for sure that it wouldn't turn into dirt, so we took the highway and Randy followed me for the first 12 miles. I was already behind on my plan by almost an hour by the time we were back on track. When we started it was 58 degrees. But by the time I hit the first break it was 65 and climbing fast.

I was frustrated but kept going, of course. South through the Everglades is SO flat. Saw a few live coral snakes and turtles, rabbits and lizards. The miles were punctuated by what my new friend Ruth called June bugs, which don't bite, but freaked me out when they would land on my hands, arms, and legs, as they are mating and at first glance look like hornets. I'm not allergic, but insect stings during exercise can cause an allergic-type reaction due to the increased blood flow and adrenaline, and a hornet bite could be serious.

The interesting thing about these small and harmless distractions was they made the time (just under 5 hours) go by quickly. The trail I was meant to have taken was under construction, and I got into a little bit of trouble for riding on a portion of it—an officer was called and I had to promise that I would never ignore the signs in the area again. Which I did not. But the new route put me back on the highway. Cycling directions kept trying to make me turn around and go to the trail. The very last 3 miles (which take on average 13-15 minutes Google kept saying to turn around and get on the trail, which it estimated would take 90+ minutes.

I kept thinking, "Go home, Google. You're drunk."

April 17- Riding day number 57 –
E.A.E—Homestead
57 miles, 135 to go

57 miles of flat felt fairly simple. The days were shorter, for sure, but starting them early as we did had the afternoons feeling fairly long.

The majority of those miles were getting into the greater Miami area, though, and traffic was more intimidating than hills for the most part. I never knew when some semi truck driver or teenager who was told to be on time 87 times was going to try and push past me in a construction zone, and close calls were frequently worse in my mind than the doubts that I'd be physically able to complete the job by that point.

Despite the traffic and increased frequency of stop lights, I was done in under 4 hours and before 10:30 AM.

We spent some time at Biscayne National Park in the afternoon, an orchid farm with an incredible koi pond, and even saw *Dumbo* to kill a little time before dinner with Tom and Dee Berry. Tom is a friend from high school who lives down there and Dee works for the Forest Service and gave us some advice on what to see in the Keys as well as listening to some of the stories from the road. It was a delightful evening, but I slept fitfully in the Airbnb that night as I looked forward to the last three days of riding, and all the bridges that began the next day.

April 18—Riding day number 58 –
Homestead—Layton
66 miles, 69 to go

Riding into the Keys was surreal. First of all, you get on a toll bridge leading to Key Largo, and we hit the bridge right at sunrise. This was the last day Randy followed me in the dark. Huge thanks again to my amazing husband. None of it would have been possible without him, least of all the nighttime riding, when I needed a pilot car.

Key Largo was incredible. Lots of animals, not much traffic at that time of morning, palm trees, shade, and pleasant ocean breeze throughout the day. When we stopped in Layton we had some key lime pie, got some rest, and planned the next day's ride. We would sleep a little later, and I would ride 52 miles to Lower Sugarloaf Key, and then a triumphant 17 miles into Key West on Saturday.

April 19—Riding day number 59 –
Layton—Big Pine Key
36 miles, 33 to go

On Thursday Dawn and a crew of six left Leesburg, GA to be there for the big finish. They drove all night and arrived on Friday shortly after I stopped riding. Mom left Boise early Friday morning, arriving in Key West late in the afternoon.

But the ride did not go quite according to plan. The first 23 miles were good, overall, although it was getting hot and I was getting tired. Fortunately not sore anymore, but I could feel the energy flagging. The Seven Mile Bridge between Marathon Key and Bahia Key was amazing. I'd been nervous about it, but I had no panic or anything. I just rode and kept riding. Six miles after I completed that, I suddenly felt my tire deflate. I didn't even realize that I'd hit something. Not having used tubes in the past two years, I almost couldn't figure out what had happened. I'd just seen Randy for a food stop at the 30 mile mark, and I texted him that I needed him to come back to pump my tire.

It is a big deal if you can't pump your tire on tubeless, and I knew I was in trouble the moment I pushed the pump even a little bit. Sealant hissed and sprayed on my legs as it sprayed through the hole where the sidewall had been punctured severely. So with 33 miles to go, I had my first legitimate flat tire of the whole cross-country trip. We decided since mom was flying into Key West, we would go toward there and see if there was a bike shop that could repair or replace the tire on short notice.

I called a few places on the island, and finally asked one of the rental places if there was someone they would recommend who might be able to fix it. They recommended Island Bicycles. I called and asked about the possibility of getting a tubeless replaced that afternoon. Dave said to bring it in and they'd see what they could do.

When they tried to inflate it, the hole sprayed sealant all over the tech, the workbench, and many of the tools. It was a very serious hole. They suggested they replace the tire, and I was concerned that it might be a few days before they could get to it, but they said they could have it done in 45 minutes or so. So we chatted about the ride, and I told them how things were going and thanked them profusely for their help. Seriously, if you're in need of a new bike or a repair and you're anywhere near Key West, go to Island Bicycles. They're the best.

We picked mom up from the airport and headed back to the Airbnb to make the finish line plans. Dawn and crew came to our place and chatted about how it would work—they had rented a second car and Dawn would meet Randy and my mom at mile 16 around 8:30, where mom would get into the car with Dawn and meet me again starting at mile 10 for the "countdown" to Key West.

April 20 Riding day number 60 –
Big Pine Key—Key West
33 miles

Seven o'clock Saturday morning I started riding where I left off on Big Pine Key. Mom and Randy were in our rental car. The bike was smooth, and it was still a little bit brisk outside from the storm that had blown through the evening before. I quickly smashed 16 miles and met Randy, Dawn, and mom at a little coffee shop on Lower Sugarloaf Key at about 8:15. Grabbed something to eat and refilled my water bottle, and was back on the bike before 8:30 with the goal of finishing before 10AM.

What felt like five minutes later, I was at mile marker 10, stopped for a picture and cutting a fabric countdown chain, and went again. The next 45 minutes were a blur of riding, honking horns and cheering, pictures at mile markers, and Facebook Live videos, with a few more than a few tears smattered along the way. I hadn't felt any pain the entire 33 miles. No heat, no foot pain, no frustration, nothing but total exhilaration.

When I was within 100 feet of Mile Marker Zero I paused and waited for Dawn to get parked so she could be part of the Live Facebook feed showing what was happening. While I was waiting, I talked to the people watching, and one of my friends said, "How's your emotions right about now?"

As I write this, it has been 14 weeks since I completed the ride, and reading that question choked me up all over again. My emotions were everywhere. I had come 3,800 miles, and in a moment I would be finished. Who even was I by this point? I choked out an answer, and Dawn got there and I finished those last 100 feet, but the questions continued to swirl in my mind as I rode the one remaining mile to Fort Zachary Taylor, where I would dip my front tire in the ocean in victory. Who does this? What did I learn? Would I do it again if I could go back in time? Was I better now? Did I feel like the same person? Would I go back to "real life" and just be the same as I was before? Would life ever be "normal" again? Would I want it to be?

*When the spirits are low, when the day appears
dark, when work becomes monotonous, when hope
hardly seems worth having, just mount a bicycle
and go out for a spin down the road, without
thought on anything but the ride you are taking.*

-Sir Arthur Conan Doyle

CHAPTER 1
THE FINISH LINE, AND BEYOND

If you're ever blessed with the opportunity to live a fantasy, be sure and take in every second of the finish line. We were taking photos at Mile Marker Zero with my mom and there was a guy leading a bike tour of Key West, and she interrupted him to tell him (and them) what I had just done, and my initial thought was, "nobody cares about this, mom...", but they did. They asked a few questions and said that was amazing, and went on their way.

Randy and the crew met me in the parking lot of Fort Zachary Taylor where we waited for mom and Dawn to get through the entrance gate, and then we paraded down to the water. I dipped my front tire in the Gulf of Mexico and the warm water lapped my bare feet. It felt phenomenal. I thought to raise my bike over my head, so I did, with a big smile across my face. I was done. Several pictures were taken and I had fun with that, and then I handed Randy the bike. As soon as he was headed back to the car with it, I had an argument in my head: One side said, "Get in the water," and the other said, "Do NOT get in the water, you're wearing tight clothes, and they'll be clingy." "GET IN THE WATER." "I'm not getting in the water. My shorts show my hips already." *"GET. IN. THE. DAMN. WATER,"* and before I could argue any further, I dove into the water. When I stood up my cheering squad was laughing, but they weren't laughing *at* me. They were laughing because it was such a joyous, spontaneous thing to do. There were hundreds of people on the beach, and the only ones looking at me were "my" people. Nobody was judging me; nobody laughing because I looked ridiculous; nobody embarrassed by or for me.

Being in that warm water in Florida and feeling so free and full of emotion reminded me of the trip we took three weeks after my dad passed away in December, 2004. It had been planned months before, and felt like a perfect respite from the emotion of the event, as well as the cold temperatures in Utah, where we were living at the time. After the funeral we invited my mom along, and during our time there, we ended up at the Nickelodeon Blast Zone splash pad in Universal Studios Orlando. They had two 500-gallon water buckets that fill about every 10 minutes or so, (but they alternate, so one dumps about every five minutes) and if you stood under them, they would tip over and drop every ounce on top of you.

My kids were having fun spraying each other with water "guns" and Randy, and I was taking pictures from a perch where I stayed mostly dry. Mom had walked tentatively to the edge of where one of the buckets was filling, and was looking up at it. Nobody dared stand right under it. It tipped over and splashed her up to her knees, and she turned away, laughing. The other bucket was filling, and she went and stood a little closer to that one. Five minutes later, she was wet to her shoulders. By this time, a crowd had started to take notice. The third time, she was directly underneath the bucket. As she raised her hands to her sides and the water came down, I cried. She was soaking it up—in her grief—and loving every second of it. There was a woman standing next to me as I took photo after photo who asked, "Do you know that woman?"

"Yes, ma'am. That's my mother."

"She's so free-spirited. I want to be like her when I grow-up!"

"She lost her husband—my father—three weeks ago."

Deep breath. "I want to be like her *now*."

After cleaning up and having some lunch and some more key lime pie (I think I had 11 pieces of pie in the three days I was in the Keys), we hung out on Key West for a little while, shopping and being tourists. It was surprising how "normal" I felt. I had just completed a multi-year event, and I didn't feel much different than I had the day before. There was quite a bit of introspection that I went through, however, and by the time we got back to our Airbnb, I could see how different I had become.

I still have bouts with anxiety and depression, but I know how to ride the waves of emotion that come with them. They are, after all, just waves, and I am an accomplished sailor on the sea. There may be waves that hit me, and hard. There are undoubtedly waves that could take me out. But I know what I have to do when they hit. Either take precautions that I am not "at sea" to begin with, or decide who I'm going to call if they hit unexpectedly. I cannot predict some of the waves, but I will not sit in the harbor just in case they are going to hit today.

When I got back to our Airbnb my brother Ethan texted me—he couldn't be there, but had wanted to share in my joy. I share his text with his permission.

Hey Jill,

There are a lot of people who talk about doing the kind of thing you've just accomplished. Something big. But as you know, there are very few who actually do them. They might think riding your bike across the country is not worth the effort or that there are more useful ways to spend your time. To be honest, sometimes I've wondered "why is Jill doing this? Is it really worth it?" Sometimes I ask myself the same questions about my own dreams, especially when I'm feeling like I'm a long way from Florida. At the end of the day, I guess you're the only one who can answer those questions for certain. But I wanted you to know that I'm proud to be your little brother. What you've done inspires me to keep working and to work even harder against the wind. I hope it leaves a permanent mark of self-confidence on your memory, something you can look to for strength for the rest of your life and beyond, an accomplishment that elevates your belief in yourself and your endless potential.

What could be more worthwhile than that? Thank you for being both a dreamer and a doer.

With love,

E

Touch down in Salt Lake City April 21, 2019 just before midnight—my bike was left with Dawn to ship home, and I was to be to work at 7AM the following morning. No rest for the wicked, as they say.

Thing is, even though I had left the area just 11 short days earlier, nothing looked familiar. d'Artagnan picked us up at the airport, and yes, I was tired, but I couldn't figure out where I was—like the buildings had been digitally enhanced while we were gone. I chalked it up to jet lag, poor lighting, and exhaustion, but when the sun came up in the morning and I was driving to work, the effect hadn't gotten any better. I drove to work and walked in the door like I had for months, but it felt very, very different. *I* felt different. I still can't explain it fully, but my theory is this: when you spend 10 years with selective blinders on, going about your day, but always with an eye toward how to get a certain thing done, and then all of a sudden those blinders are removed, the world looks completely changed.

When I posted the photo above on Facebook, my friend and fellow author Leta Greene (*How to Embrace Your Inner Hotness, Love, Me Too*) shared my post with this comment added: *Meet Jillyn Hawkley Peterson. She got this idea to ride her bike from coast to coast.*

That's a pretty bold thing to do. Here's what's so cool about this, she is not a professional rider, she didn't get paid to do this, she wanted to. She used this to push back her "cant's" And "fears" in life. She's a normal person just like you and me. She has reasons she could have been like "no way! I can't do that!" Instead, she has used those things to fuel her ride. She has been open about how she suffers from anxiety, and she has a normal woman's body that has had babies— but look LOOK at her strength the perfection in her imperfection. This is Hot!

I also placed this photo as my backdrop on my work computer.

From my Facebook post May 7, 2019 (two weeks post-finish)

"Well, it took two weeks of me seeing this photo for it to happen.

The itty bitty (insert rhyming expletive here) committee (IBSC) in my head barged in during a moment of waiting for a file to upload, with its criticisms.

"You really posted this for all your friends to see? You should have put on something to cover your..."

I shut it up pretty quickly as the file got finished, but that self-doubt and irritation at allowing myself to be vulnerable with all my body issues on display ended up getting the better of me later in the day yesterday.

So I sat with this picture for a few minutes, but objectively. Please know that I am not posting this for compliments. I feel like of all the people in the world, my friends will understand. Maybe you have been in my shoes.

When I look at this picture I see a strong, imperfect body, and messy hair, indicating days of work and literal blood, sweat, tears, and spit spread across literally thousands of miles of roads. I see the absolute joy I felt in that moment, but also in the moment I'd had every riding day when I took my shoes off. I see the incredible feeling of having followed a monumentally challenging feat through to completion. I see the hat Randy got me because he loves how beautiful a blue hat on a girl with a blonde ponytail looks. I see the agony of 1,200-foot climbs and the terrifying thrill of realizing if I hit a pebble at 50+ mph, it may not kill me, but I will wish it had.

I hope the IBSC stays adjourned for a long time. But when it comes back, I hope I will remember to look at this picture.

It is me.

It is real.

I am alive (and barefoot) and I love it."

PROLOGUE:

You only die once. If you're doing it well, you get to live every day. So be in the pictures, hips and all. Be joyous, even if your hair is a mess; even if you didn't shave your armpits that morning; even if you have a scar on your leg that you don't like; even if *everybody* is watching. Don't erase your joys. Don't not feel your sorrows in order to make others more comfortable with your grief. Feel it, even if experiencing the pain of it makes you think it will swallow you whole. Hold someone's hand, or let them hug you, and let them take some of the weight from your shoulders. People who know your struggle are rejoicing or crying with you. People who love you are proud and pleased that you made it; those on earth and those waiting in the wings for you to cross over. If you want to get in the water, GET IN THE WATER. There is nothing wrong with being so full of emotion that you want to immerse yourself in the experience.

My other lesson for anyone who will listen: If you have found this epoch inspiring, please know that I am pretty normal. I have doubts and fears, anxiety and depression. I have a house payment and drive a thirteen-year-old car, and a pretty normal job. I'm not independently wealthy, a natural athlete, or someone who trained with professionals to do this.

Whenever people said, "I could never do anything like that!" to me, I thanked them for their praise, but I also reminded them that cycling and endurance sports aren't for everybody.

They aren't *supposed* to be. But the cool thing is that I found something that lit me up, and I went for it—and lest you think it was positivity and optimism that got it done, it was not. I didn't even catch a *glimpse* of success until Hattiesburg, Mississippi. I knew what it looked like, sure. I knew that it was possible for *somebody* to do it, I just knew it wouldn't be me. I'd quit or get hurt or die first.

If I thought I should always be as cheery as I was on Day One and always just *love* getting on the bike, discouragement kicking in would have ended the ride. I embraced the pain, discouragement, and fear. I didn't try to kill it or hurt it or even shame it. I invited it along for the ride.

I asked for encouragement from friends. I took it wherever I could find it, but I also didn't ignore the doubts. The more you resist the doubt, the bigger it gets. The more you try and suck it up and just work through it, the more likely it is to swallow you up. *I* could never do it—until I did. Remember heartbreaker hill on Day One? I was no more a champion on April 20, 2019 than I was on May 27, 2017, but I got on the bike and I rode. "...by all means paint, and that voice will be silenced."

Please, dear reader—find something that lights *you* up inside. That truly, honestly, without rhyme, reason, or any visible logic, makes you so excited and scared and brain-mushed spinning in circles that you are telling your spouse, friends, neighbors, the cashier at the grocery store, and anybody who will listen what you plan to do. Tell them about your hopes. Make solid plans. Make them again. Then make them again, and when you think you're never going to be ready to begin based on where you started thinking about it and how far you have to go to get there, get started.

Don't wait. Bring your fears and doubts with you. You will fail, most likely. Probably early. Keep failing forward. Trip as often as you must. Get up as often as you fall. Take care of yourself, but don't be so easy on yourself that you lose the light that got you there in the first place. Keep your "team" on board—whatever that takes. If it's cycling, great. If it's singing, awesome. If it's cutting hair or splitting wood or driving race cars or running or chainsaw wood carving or blowing glass or oil painting or software development or breeding labradoodles or landscaping or becoming the mayor of your town or public speaking or designing shoes or teaching math or history or photography or driving Uber or antiquing or restoring old cars or organizing closets or scrapbooking—if it makes you so happy you can't believe you *get* to do it, even when you think it is too hard? DO. IT.

Expect the resistance and the fears and the doubt and everything to come up. Don't let the simplicity or complexity stop you from doing something you want to do. Ever. Don't wait until the timing is perfect. It will *never be perfect*. Make *your* lifetime—*your WHOLE lifetime*—a lifetime of adventure. *LIVE* this moment. Do not wait until AnOther Day. Putting off your happiness until you reach some magical space that exists only in your mind will *NEVER* have you achieving a single worthwhile goal.

My dad died just two months and six days after his 60th birthday. I was fortunate that a few weeks before he passed I was inspired to write him a thank-you note for something he did for me when I was 12 years old that I have never forgotten. I will forever remember the feeling I had when I got the call that he was gone—yes, I was very sad. But in the briefest moment between gasps of sobbing, I had the most peaceful thought: I have no regrets in this relationship. Nothing was left unsaid. He knew how much I love him, and I know how much he loves me.

I have tried to bring this thought into my relationships as often as possible since his passing—leave as many positive interactions as you can. Love with all your heart. Be where you want to be. Look at them like they may be gone tomorrow—because truly, they may. Tell them you want nothing more than to be with them right now, at this moment. Celebrate *them* every time you can, if you are able. Know that one day when you do that, it will be the very last time you get to celebrate with them. Make it count. Everybody you know is only going to die once. We need to stop acting like they (and we) will be around forever simply because they always have been.

If tomorrow never comes for me, or for you, please know this: I love you. I want you to be happy, *RIGHT NOW*. I know that whatever deity you pray to or choose to believe or not believe in loves you. I know that life is short, and scary, and intimidating. But I also know that you are stronger, better, brighter, smarter, more wonderful than you can imagine. You *can* do the hard thing you think would be cool to do. You *will* do amazing things. I, and an audience of thousands, applaud your every figurative pedal stroke, even if you can't hear us, see us, or even know we exist. You are wonderful, you are worthy, and you are enough.

My mother, for my 50th birthday, which happened to coincide with Easter Sunday 2019, purchased two small paintings in a shop on Key West. One is the Mile Marker 0 sign on one side of the street corner, that says END, and the other is the Mile Marker 0 sign on the other side of the street corner that says, BEGIN. She wanted me to remember that while this signifies the end of one journey, it begins another. I hope to see you on whichever roads you choose to ride. You've got this, and I'm cheering for you all the way.

BEGIN

DRABATIC PRESS

Note to Authors (including teen authors): As a new press, we are seeking works of fiction for our list. If you believe you've written something we should see, please send us a message in a bottle. Or an email, if that's how you roll.

We offer quite a different experience from a traditional publisher, or even a small press:

> ➤ We do not acquire your copyright. We buy only first-publication rights. All subsequent publishing, rights, in whatever form, remain with the author.

> ➤ We build client lists and share those client lists across authors. All our authors benefit from cross-marketing with other authors in our troupe.

> ➤ We share purchase data. As a Drabatic Press author, you will know who is buying your books, not just how many you're selling. Every sale augments your marketing list.

> ➤ Our royalty structure beats even self-publishing, especially through Amazon.

> ➤ We have a teen division, consisting of books published *by teen authors*.

If any or all of the above sounds like an improvement on what you are currently doing, or if you have a work you'd like to run by the acquiring editors at Drabatic, please contact us.

Drabatic Press, LLC.
drabaticpress@gmail.com

Also Available at DrabaticPress.com:

Ever wonder why your phone messages don't get returned? Why your texts always get read the wrong way? Why everything you say on Facebook creates an argument?

You can stop wondering. This book will tell you. If you're a businessman, a salesman, or just want to understand what's going on in social media, this book is for you. By Chris Jones, author of *From Poop to Gold, The Marketing Magic of the Harmon Brothers*.

Speaking of which, Drabatic Press Recommends:

Author Chris Jones pulls back the curain and reveals the behind-the-scened magid of one of America's most successful advertising companies—responsible for Squatty Potty, Chatbooks, Purple, Poo-Pourri, Lume, Shapermint, and dozens of others, totaling hundreds of millions of views and millions in sales. An in-depth look at the creative process that continually churns out viral hits.

Available at harmonbrothersbook.com

Made in the USA
Lexington, KY
07 December 2019

58272913R00102